25TH ANNIVERSARY EDITION

THE 21 IRREFUTABLE
LAWS OF
LEADERSHIP
WORKBOOK

REVISED AND UPDATED

FOLLOW THEM AND PEOPLE WILL FOLLOW YOU

JOHN C.
MAXWELL

HARPERCOLLINS
LEADERSHIP

AN IMPRINT OF HARPERCOLLINS

The 21 Irrefutable Laws of Leadership Workbook 25th Anniversary Edition

© 2002, 2007, 2022 by John C. Maxwell

ISBN 978-0-310-15949-0 (softcover)

ISBN 978-0-310-16038-0 (ebook)

Published by HarperCollins Leadership, an imprint of HarperCollins Focus LLC.

Published in association with Yates & Yates, www.yates2.com.

Scripture quotations marked CEV are taken from the Contemporary English Version. Copyright © 1991, 1992, 1995 by American Bible Society. Used by permission.

Scripture quotations marked *The Message* are taken from THE MESSAGE. Copyright © 1993, 2002, 2018 by Eugene H. Peterson. Used by permission of NavPress. All rights reserved. Represented by Tyndale House Publishers, Inc.

Any internet addresses, phone numbers, or company or product information printed in this book are offered as a resource and are not intended in any way to be or to imply an endorsement by HarperCollins Leadership, nor does HarperCollins Leadership vouch for the existence, content, or services of these sites, phone numbers, companies, or products beyond the life of this book.

First Printing August 2022 / Printed in the United States of America

24 25 26 27 28 LBC 6 5 4 3 2

CONTENTS

Introduction ix

21 Laws Leadership Evaluation xv

1. THE LAW OF THE LID 1

How Well You Lead Determines How Well You Succeed

Brothers Dick and Maurice came as close as they could to living the American Dream—without making it. Instead a guy named Ray did it with the company they had founded. It happened because they didn't know the Law of the Lid.

2. THE LAW OF INFLUENCE 13

The True Measure of Leadership Is Influence—Nothing More, Nothing Less

Abraham Lincoln started with the rank of captain, but by the time the war was over, he was a private. What happened? He was a casualty of the Law of Influence.

3. THE LAW OF PROCESS 23

Leadership Develops Daily, Not in a Day

Theodore Roosevelt helped create a world power, won a Nobel Peace Prize, and became president of the United States. But today you wouldn't even know his name if he hadn't known the Law of Process.

4. THE LAW OF NAVIGATION 33

Anyone Can Steer the Ship, but It Takes a Leader to Chart the Course

Using a fail-safe compass, Scott led his team of adventurers to the end of the earth—and to inglorious deaths. They would have lived if only he, their leader, had known the Law of Navigation.

5. THE LAW OF ADDITION... 43

Leaders Add Value by Serving Others

What kind of a Fortune 500 CEO works on a folding table, answers his own phone, visits hourly employees as often as possible, and is criticized by Wall Street for being too good to his employees? The kind of leader who understands the Law of Addition.

6. THE LAW OF SOLID GROUND.......................... 53

Trust Is the Foundation of Leadership

If only Robert McNamara had known the Law of Solid Ground, the war in Vietnam—and everything that happened at home because of it—might have turned out differently.

7. THE LAW OF RESPECT................................. 65

People Naturally Follow Better Leaders Than Themselves

The odds were stacked against her in just about every possible way, but thousands and thousands of people called her their leader. Why? Because they could not escape the power of the Law of Respect.

8. THE LAW OF INTUITION.............................. 79

Leaders Evaluate Everything with a Leadership Bias

When Jamie Kern Lima created a makeup line that worked for women with skin conditions, no one would carry it. She was even told no one would buy beauty products from someone who looked like her. But because she followed the Law of Intuition, she became a billionaire.

9. THE LAW OF MAGNETISM 91

Who You Are Is Who You Attract

How does the new young CEO resurrect a formerly respected one-hundred-year-old brand and make it successful again? She leverages her knowledge of the Law of Magnetism.

10. THE LAW OF CONNECTION 101

Leaders Touch a Heart Before They Ask for a Hand

Who would take out a full-page ad in a national newspaper on Boss's Day to thank their CEO? Employees who've been touched by a leader who lives the Law of Connection.

11. THE LAW OF THE INNER CIRCLE. 111

Those Closest to You Determine the Level of Your Success

No leaders—past, present, or future—are successful without this. It will either make or break them. What am I referring to? It's none other than the Law of the Inner Circle.

12. THE LAW OF EMPOWERMENT. 121

Only Secure Leaders Give Power to Others

Henry Ford is considered an icon of American business for revolutionizing the automobile industry. So what caused him to stumble so badly that his son feared Ford Motor Company would go out of business? He was held captive by the Law of Empowerment.

13. THE LAW OF THE PICTURE 133

People Do What People See

Easy Company withstood the German advance at the Battle of the Bulge and dashed Hitler's last hope for stopping the Allies' advance. They were able to do it because their leaders embraced the Law of the Picture.

14. THE LAW OF BUY-IN 145

People Buy into the Leader, Then the Vision

They freed their nation by passively protesting, even when it cost them their lives by the thousands. What would inspire them to do such a thing? The Law of Buy-In.

15. THE LAW OF VICTORY 155

Leaders Find Ways for the Team to Win

What saved England from the Blitz, broke apartheid's back in South Africa, and won the Chicago Bulls multiple world championships? In all three cases the answer is the same. Their leaders lived by the Law of Victory.

16. THE LAW OF THE BIG MO 163

Momentum Is a Leader's Best Friend

Jaime Escalante has been called the best teacher in America. But his teaching ability is only half the story. His and Garfield High School's success came because of the Law of the Big Mo.

17. THE LAW OF PRIORITIES 175

Leaders Understand That Activity Is Not Necessarily Accomplishment

They called him the wizard. His priorities were so focused that if you gave him a date and time, he could have told you exactly what drill his players were performing and why! It won him ten championships. What can the Law of Priorities do for you?

18. THE LAW OF SACRIFICE 185

A Leader Must Give Up to Go Up

What would you give up for the people who followed you? This leader gave his life. Why? Because he understood the power of the Law of Sacrifice.

19. THE LAW OF TIMING 195

When to Lead Is As Important As What to Do and Where to Go

Leaders at every level dropped the ball: the mayor, the governor, the cabinet secretary, and the president. Not one of them understood the potential devastation that can come when a leader violates the Law of Timing.

20. THE LAW OF EXPLOSIVE GROWTH 205

To Add Growth, Lead Followers—To Multiply, Lead Leaders

Is it possible to train more than a million people around the globe? It is if you use leader's math. That's the secret of the Law of Explosive Growth.

21. THE LAW OF LEGACY

21. THE LAW OF LEGACY 219

A Leader's Lasting Value Is Measured by Succession

What will people say at your funeral? The things they say tomorrow depend on how you live today using the Law of Legacy.

Conclusion 229

Suggestions for Leadership Growth 231

Notes 239

INTRODUCTION

Every book is a conversation between the author and the individual reading it. Some people pick up a book hoping for a bit of encouragement. Some devour a book's information as if they were attending an intensive seminar. Others find in its pages a mentor they can meet with on a daily, weekly, or monthly basis.

The thing I love about writing books is that it allows me to "talk" to many people I will never personally meet. That's why I made the decision in 1977 to become an author. I had a passion to add value to people that energized me to write. That passion still burns within me today. Few things are more rewarding to me than being on the road and having someone I've never met approach me to say, "Thank you. Your books have really helped me." It's why I write—and intend to continue writing!

Despite the deep satisfaction of knowing that my books help people, there is also a great frustration that comes with being an author. Once a book is published, it freezes in time. If you and I knew each other personally and we met weekly or monthly to talk about leadership, every time we got together I'd share with you something new I'd learned. As a person, I continue to grow. I'm constantly reading. I'm analyzing my mistakes. I'm talking to excellent leaders to learn from them. Each time you and I were to sit down, I'd say, "You won't believe what I just learned."

As a conference and event speaker, I often teach the principles I write about in my books, and I'm constantly updating my material. I use new stories. I refine ideas. And I often gain new insights as I stand in front of an audience. However, when I go back to books that I've written previously, I first become aware of how I've changed since I've written them. But second, I become frustrated because the books can't grow and change along with me.

When my publisher asked if I would like to revise *The 21 Irrefutable Laws of Leadership* for its tenth anniversary, I got excited. When I originally wrote the book, it was my answer to the question, "If you were to take everything you've learned about leadership over the years and boil it down into a short list of laws, what would they be?" I put on paper the essentials of leadership, communicated as simply and clearly as possible. And soon after the book was published and it appeared on bestseller lists, I realized it had the potential to help a lot of people become better leaders. Ten years later, I was able to add what I'd learned during the previous decade. There were two new laws I had discovered and two old ones I realized were subsets of other laws. I was glad to make those updates plus others. It was my chance to improve the book and workbook.

GROWTH = CHANGE

Another fifteen years has gone by since then. When my publisher asked if I wanted to revisit the book and update it again for this twenty-fifth anniversary edition, I of course said yes. However, as I approached the task, I wondered how I would feel about the laws and what I would want to change. I'm happy to say that when I reread the book, I recognized the laws were as solid as ever! They continue to stand the test of time. If you follow them, then people will follow you.

While teaching the laws for more than two decades in dozens of countries around the world, I fielded thousands of questions about the laws. That process advanced my thinking beyond what it was when I first wrote the book or did the tenth anniversary revision. Working on this twenty-fifth anniversary edition has allowed me to make more improvements from my experience leading others and teaching the laws. For example, I slightly reworded the tag lines for the Law of the Lid, the Law of Respect, and the Law of the Inner Circle to make them clearer. I removed some of the stories that felt dated and replaced them with stories about fantastic leaders such as Angela Ahrendts, Ed Bastian, Jamie Kern Lima, and Mark Cole. And I developed new material to better explain and illustrate some of the laws. I would estimate that I revised 30 percent of the book and streamlined some of it too.

There are two other things that have been confirmed for me as I've taught the 21 Laws over the years and revisited the book:

1. LEADERSHIP REQUIRES THE ABILITY TO DO MORE THAN ONE THING

Instinctively, successful people understand that focus is important to achievement. But leadership is very complex. During a break at a conference where I was teaching the

21 Laws, a young college student came up to me and said, "I know you are teaching 21 Laws of Leadership, but I want to get to the bottom line." With intensity, he raised his index finger and asked, "What is the one thing I need to know about leadership?"

Trying to match his intensity, I raised my index finger and answered, "The one thing you need to know about leadership is that there is more than one thing you need to know about leadership!" To lead well, we must do 21 things well.

2. No One Does All 21 Laws Well

Despite the fact that we must do 21 things well to be excellent leaders, the reality is that none of us does all of them well. For example, I am average or below average in five of the laws—and I wrote the book! So what is a leader to do? Ignore those laws? No, develop a leadership team.

At the beginning of this workbook, there is a leadership evaluation. I encourage you to take it to evaluate your aptitude for each law. Once you've discovered in which laws you are average or below, begin looking for team members whose skills are strong where yours are weak. They will complement you and vice versa, and the whole team will benefit. That will make it possible for you to develop an all-star leadership team. Remember, none of us is as smart as all of us.

SOME THINGS CHANGE— OTHERS NEVER DO

Leadership has certainly become more complex in recent years. The times are difficult, and it can be challenging to lead people to work together. The need for good leadership has never been greater. Businesses, government, families, communities, and teams are crying out for good leaders to help them. That's why I'm especially excited to introduce a new generation of leaders to these laws. Learn the laws, and they will help you to lead. While the particular leadership challenges change from year to year and from community to community, some things have not changed. It's still true that leadership is leadership, no matter where you go or what you do. Times change. Technology marches forward. Cultures differ from place to place. But the principles of leadership are constant—whether you're looking at the citizens of ancient Greece, the Hebrews in the Old Testament, the armies of the modern world, the leaders in the international community, the pastors in local churches, or the businesspeople of today's global economy. The laws of leadership apply regardless of the gender, age, experience, or environment of the leader. The laws of leadership are unchanging and stand the test of time.

As you work through the following lessons, I'd like you to keep in mind . . .

1. The laws can be learned. Some are easier to understand and apply than others, but every one of them can be acquired.
2. The laws can stand alone. **Each law complements all the others, but you don't need one in order to learn another.**
3. The laws carry consequences with them. Apply the laws, and people will follow you. Violate or ignore them, and you will not be effective leading others.
4. The laws are timeless. Whether you're young or old, inexperienced or experienced, the laws apply. They applied to your grandparents, and they will apply to your great-grandchildren.
5. The laws are the foundation of leadership. Once you learn the principles, you will have to practice them and apply them to your life. If you do, you will be a better leader.

Whether you are a follower who is just beginning to discover the impact of leadership, or you're a natural leader who already has followers, you can become a better leader. Whether you are in your teens leading others in student government or sports, or you are in your seventies like I am making a difference in your later years, you can improve. As you read about the laws, you may recognize that you already practice some of them very effectively. Other laws may expose weaknesses you didn't know you had. Use your interaction with the laws as a learning experience and complete the exercises at the end of each lesson to help you apply each law to your life.

You can certainly learn the laws of leadership on your own using this workbook. However, since leadership is about working with people, this workbook has been set up so that groups can learn about the laws together. The first three sections in each lesson (Read, Observe, Learn) are to be completed individually, and the last three sections (Discuss, Apply, Action) are most effective if reviewed in a group setting. Since individuals have different strengths and weaknesses, if you work together on each law, you will learn from each other. *Before you get started working through the lessons, I recommend that you take the leadership evaluation,* which you will find on the next few pages. This will give you a benchmark of where you are starting in the leadership growth process. Then, when you are done with this workbook, complete the evaluation again.

No matter where you are in the leadership development process, know this: the greater the number of laws you learn, the better leader you will become. Each law is like a tool, ready to be picked up and used to help you achieve your dreams and add value to other people. Pick up even one, and you will become a better leader. Learn them all, and people will gladly follow you.

Now, let's open the toolbox together.

21 LAWS LEADERSHIP EVALUATION

Read each statement below and score yourself for each, using the following scale:

0 Never
1 Rarely
2 Occasionally
3 Always

1. THE LAW OF THE LID
How Well You Lead Determines How Well You Succeed

___ a) When faced with a challenge, my first thought is, *Who can I enlist to help? not What can I do?*

___ b) When my team, department, or organization fails to achieve an objective, my first assumption is that it's some kind of leadership issue.

___ c) I believe that developing my leadership skills will increase my effectiveness dramatically.

___ TOTAL +1 = ___ Your Score

2. THE LAW OF INFLUENCE
The True Measure of Leadership Is Influence—Nothing More, Nothing Less

___ a) I rely on influence rather than on my position or title to get others to follow me or do what I want.

___ b) During discussions or brainstorming settings, people turn to me and ask for my advice.

___ c) I rely on my relationships with others rather than organizational systems and procedures to get things done.

___ TOTAL +1 = ___ Your Score

3. THE LAW OF PROCESS
Leadership Develops Daily, Not in a Day

___ a) I have a concrete, specific plan for personal growth that I engage in weekly.

___ b) I have found experts and mentors for key areas of my life with whom I engage on a regular basis.

___ c) To promote my professional growth, I have read at least six books (*or* taken at least one worthwhile class *or* listened to twelve or more audio lessons) per year for the last three years.

___ TOTAL +1 = ___ Your Score

4. THE LAW OF NAVIGATION
Anyone Can Steer the Ship, but It Takes a Leader to Chart the Course

___ a) I spot problems, obstacles, and trends that will impact the outcome of initiatives the organization puts into place.

___ b) I can clearly see a pathway for the implementation of a vision, including not only the process but also the people and resources needed.

___ c) I am asked to plan initiatives for my team, department, or organization.

___ TOTAL +1 = ___ Your Score

5. THE LAW OF ADDITION
Leaders Add Value by Serving Others

___ a) Rather than being annoyed when team members have issues preventing them from doing their jobs effectively, I see the issues as an opportunity to serve and help those people.

___ b) I clear away obstacles and look for ways to make things better for the people I lead.

___ c) I find great personal satisfaction in helping other people become more successful.

___ TOTAL +1 = ___ Your Score

6. THE LAW OF SOLID GROUND

Trust Is the Foundation of Leadership

___ a) The people I work with confide in me regarding sensitive issues and future plans.

___ b) When I tell people in the organization that I will do something, they can count on me to follow through.

___ c) I avoid undermining others or talking behind their backs.

___ TOTAL +1 = ___ Your Score

7. THE LAW OF RESPECT

People Naturally Follow Better Leaders Than Themselves

___ a) People are naturally drawn to me and often want to do things with me just to spend time with me.

___ b) People I work with gladly take my suggestions and follow my direction.

___ c) I make courageous decisions and take personal risks to benefit my team members even if there is no benefit to me.

___ TOTAL +1 = ___ Your Score

8. THE LAW OF INTUITION

Leaders Evaluate Everything with a Leadership Bias

___ a) I can easily gauge morale, whether in a room full of people, on a team, or in the greater organization.

___ b) I often take the right action as a leader even if I cannot explain why.

___ c) I can read situations and sense trends without having to gather a lot of hard evidence.

___ TOTAL +1 = ___ Your Score

9. THE LAW OF MAGNETISM

Who You Are Is Who You Attract

___ a) I am satisfied with the caliber of people who report to me.

___ b) I expect the people I attract to be similar to me in values, skills, and leadership ability.

___ c) I recognize that no personnel process can improve the quality of people I recruit compared to improving myself.

___ TOTAL +1 = ____ Your Score

10. THE LAW OF CONNECTION

Leaders Touch a Heart Before They Ask for a Hand

___ a) When I am new to a team, one of the first things I try to do is to develop a personal connection with everyone.

___ b) I know the stories, hopes, and dreams of the people I lead.

___ c) I avoid asking people to help accomplish the vision until we have built a relationship that goes beyond the nuts and bolts of our work together.

___ TOTAL +1 = ____ Your Score

11. THE LAW OF THE INNER CIRCLE

Those Closest to You Determine the Level of Your Success

___ a) I am strategic and highly selective about which people are closest to me personally and professionally.

___ b) I regularly rely on some key people in my life to help accomplish my goals.

___ c) I believe that 50 percent or more of the credit for my accomplishments goes to the people on my team.

___ TOTAL +1 = ____ Your Score

12. THE LAW OF EMPOWERMENT

Only Secure Leaders Give Power to Others

____ a) No matter how talented the people who work for me, I don't feel threatened by them.

____ b) It is my regular practice to give people I lead the authority to make decisions and take risks.

____ c) I genuinely celebrate when someone from my team is recognized by others or promoted to a higher position.

____ TOTAL +1 = ____ Your Score

13. THE LAW OF THE PICTURE

People Do What People See

____ a) If I observe an undesirable action or quality in team members, I check to make sure I'm not guilty of it myself before addressing it with them.

____ b) I am continually working to make sure my values, words, and actions are consistent with one another.

____ c) I do what I should rather than what I want because I am conscious that I am setting an example for others.

____ TOTAL +1 = ____ Your Score

14. THE LAW OF BUY-IN

People Buy into the Leader, Then the Vision

____ a) I recognize that a lack of credibility *in* leaders can be as harmful to an organization as a lack of vision *from* leaders.

____ b) When members of my team don't follow my direction, I examine whether I have a credibility problem before assuming they have a compliance problem.

____ c) Even when my ideas are not great, my people tend to give me the benefit of the doubt and work with me.

____ TOTAL +1 = ____ Your Score

15. THE LAW OF VICTORY
Leaders Find Ways for the Team to Win

____ a) When I lead a team, I feel ultimate responsibility for whether it achieves its goals.

____ b) I am continually looking for ways to help members of the team achieve victory.

____ c) I make personal sacrifices to help ensure victory for my team, department, or organization.

____ TOTAL +1 = ____ Your Score

16. THE LAW OF THE BIG MO
Momentum Is a Leader's Best Friend

____ a) I am aware of the morale of my team and take responsibility for trying to keep it high.

____ b) Whenever I make a major leadership decision, I consider how that decision will impact momentum in my team, department, or organization.

____ c) I initiate specific actions with the purpose of generating momentum when introducing something new or controversial.

____ TOTAL +1 = ____ Your Score

17. THE LAW OF PRIORITIES
Leaders Understand That Activity Is Not Necessarily Accomplishment

____ a) I avoid tasks that do not require my personal leadership, don't have a tangible return, or don't reward me personally.

____ b) I set aside time daily, monthly, and yearly to plan my upcoming schedule and activities based on my priorities.

____ c) I delegate any task for which a team member can be at least 80 percent as effective as I could be doing it.

____ TOTAL +1 = ____ Your Score

18. THE LAW OF SACRIFICE

A Leader Must Give Up to Go Up

___ a) I know making trade-offs is a natural part of leadership growth, and I make sacrifices to become a better leader as long as they don't violate my values.

___ b) I expect to give more than my followers do in order to accomplish the vision.

___ c) I will focus on responsibilities and give up my rights to reach my potential as a leader.

___ TOTAL +1 = ___ Your Score

19. THE LAW OF TIMING

When to Lead Is As Important As What to Do and Where to Go

___ a) I expend as much effort figuring out the timing for an initiative as I do the strategy.

___ b) When I know the timing is right for an initiative, I will launch it rather than waiting while trying to develop the ideal strategy.

___ c) I can sense whether people are ready for an idea.

___ TOTAL +1 = ___ Your Score

20. THE LAW OF EXPLOSIVE GROWTH

To Add Growth, Lead Followers—To Multiply, Lead Leaders

___ a) I believe that I can grow my organization more rapidly by developing leaders than by any other method.

___ b) I spend a significant amount of time every week investing in the development of the top 20 percent of my leaders.

___ c) I would rather see leaders I develop succeed out on their own than keep them with me so that I can keep mentoring them.

___ TOTAL +1 = ___ Your Score

21. THE LAW OF LEGACY
A Leader's Lasting Value Is Measured by Succession

___ a) I possess a strong sense of why I am in my job and why I am leading.

___ b) In each position I've held, I have identified people who can carry on after me, and I have invested in them.

___ c) One of my strongest motivations is to leave any team I lead better than I found it.

___ TOTAL +1 = ___ Your Score

Now that you have completed the evaluation, examine each law and note your strengths and weaknesses. Use the following guidelines to help you proceed.

8–9 This law is in your strength zone. Make the most of this skill and mentor others in this area.

5–7 Target this law for growth. You have potential to make it a strength.

0–4 This is a weakness. Hire staff with this strength or partner with others in this area.

After you have examined the score for each law to determine your strength in that area, total all 21 scores in the left blank and divide by 21 to find your average leadership score. If you desire to determine your score on a scale from 1 to 10, then add all 21 scores in the right blank and divide by 21. Record your overall score below.

___ Overall Average

1

THE LAW OF THE LID

How Well You Lead Determines
How Well You Succeed

The Law of the Lid will help you understand the value of leadership. If you can get a handle on this law, you will see the incredible impact of leadership on every aspect of life.

READ

In 1930, two young brothers named Dick and Maurice moved from New Hampshire to California in search of the American Dream. They had just gotten out of high school, and they saw few opportunities back home. So they headed straight for Hollywood where they eventually found jobs on a movie studio set.

After a while, their entrepreneurial spirit and interest in the entertainment industry prompted them to open a theater in Glendale, a town about five miles northeast of Hollywood. But despite all their efforts, the brothers just couldn't make the business profitable.

The brothers' desire for success was strong, so they kept looking for better business opportunities. Drive-in restaurants were a new phenomenon springing up in the early thirties as people became more dependent on cars. Rather than eating in a dining room, customers placed orders with carhops and received their food on trays, right in their cars. Back then, food was served on dinner plates complete with glassware and metal utensils.

In 1937, Dick and Maurice opened a small drive-in restaurant in Pasadena, and it was a great success. In 1940, they decided to move the operation to San Bernardino, a working-class boomtown fifty miles east of Los Angeles, built a larger facility, and expanded their menu from hot dogs, fries, and shakes to include barbecued beef and pork sandwiches, hamburgers, and other items. Their business exploded. Annual sales reached $200,000, and the brothers found themselves splitting $50,000 in profits every year—a sum that put them in the town's financial elite.

In 1948, their intuition told them that times were changing. They eliminated the carhops, started serving only walk-up customers, and streamlined everything to reduce their costs and lower their prices. They reduced their menu and put their focus on selling hamburgers. They eliminated plates, glassware, and metal utensils, switching to paper products instead.

They also created what they called the Speedy Service System. Their kitchen became like an assembly line, where each employee focused on service with speed. The brothers' goal was to fill each customer's order in thirty seconds or less. And they succeeded. By the mid-1950s, annual revenue hit $350,000, and by then, Dick and Maurice split net profits of about $100,000 each year.

Who were these brothers? You've probably already guessed their last name: *McDonald*. Dick and Maurice McDonald had hit the great American jackpot, and the rest, as they say, is history, right? Wrong. The McDonalds never went any farther because their leadership put a lid on their ability to succeed.

It's true that the McDonald brothers were financially secure. Theirs was one of the most profitable restaurant enterprises in the country, and they felt that they had a hard time spending all the money they made. Their genius was in customer service and kitchen organization. In fact, their talent was so widely known in food service circles that people started writing them and visiting their restaurant from all over the country to learn more about their methods. At one point, they received as many as three hundred calls and letters every month.

That led them to the idea of marketing the McDonald's concept. The idea of franchising restaurants wasn't new. It had been around for several decades. To the McDonald brothers, it looked like a way to make money without having to open another restaurant themselves. In 1952, they got started, but their effort was a dismal failure. The reason was simple. They lacked the leadership necessary to make a larger enterprise effective. Dick and Maurice were good single-restaurant owners. They understood how to run a business, make their systems efficient, cut costs, and increase profits. They were efficient managers, but they were not great leaders. Their thinking patterns clamped a lid down on what they could do and become. At the height of their success, Dick and Maurice found themselves smack-dab against the Law of the Lid.

Then in 1954, the brothers met Ray Kroc. He had been running a small company that sold machines for making milk shakes. Kroc knew the McDonald brothers because their restaurant was one of his best customers. After visiting their store, he had a vision for its potential: he could see the restaurant going nationwide in hundreds of markets. He soon struck a deal with Dick and Maurice, and in 1955, he formed McDonald's Systems, Inc. (later called the McDonald's Corporation).

In the years that Dick and Maurice McDonald had attempted to franchise their food service system, they managed to sell the concept to just fifteen buyers, only ten of whom actually opened restaurants. And even in that size enterprise, their limited leadership and vision were hindrances. For example, when their first franchisee, Neil Fox of Phoenix, told the brothers that he wanted to call his restaurant McDonald's, Dick's response was, "What . . . for? McDonald's means nothing in Phoenix."

Kroc thought—and led—differently. He immediately bought the rights to a franchise so that he could use it as a model and prototype so that he could sell franchises to others. Between 1955 and 1959, Kroc succeeded in opening one hundred restaurants. Four years after that, there were five hundred McDonald's restaurants. During his first eight years with McDonald's, he took no salary and borrowed money from the bank and against his life insurance to help cover the salaries of a few key leaders he wanted on the team. He had the vision and ability to make McDonald's a nationwide entity. And in 1961 for the sum of $2.7 million, Kroc bought the exclusive rights to McDonald's from the brothers, and he proceeded to turn it into an American institution and global entity. Today McDonald's has opened more than 38,000 restaurants in 120 countries.[1]

OBSERVE

Leadership ability is the lid that determines a person's level of effectiveness. The lower an individual's ability to lead, the lower the lid on his potential. The higher the individual's ability to lead, the higher the lid on his potential. Leadership ability—or more specifically the lack of leadership ability—was the lid on the McDonald brothers' effectiveness.

1 What are two steps that Ray Kroc took to build the franchise business that the McDonald bothers didn't take?

_____

_____

_____

_____

_____

_____

2 How did these actions reflect Ray Kroc's leadership ability?

_____

_____

_____

_____

_____

_____

3 From your profession or area of service, give an example of a leader who has been limited by his or her "lid." How has this leader's "lid" affected the organization?

_____

_____

_____

_____

_____

_____

4 Do you know someone whose leadership lid seems unlimited?

_____

_____

_____

_____

_____

LEARN

Whatever you will accomplish is restricted by your ability to lead others. Let me give you a picture of what I mean. Hold your left hand out in front of you, palm down. That represents your leadership level. If your leadership is low, hold your hand down at waist level. If it's average, hold it chest high. Now put out your right hand below it. That's your success. Here's the reality of leadership and success. Your success hand can *never* go higher than your leadership hand. It will always bump up against it.

I'll explain it another way. Let's say that when it comes to success, you're an 8 (on a scale from 1 to 10). That's pretty good. I think it would be safe to say that the McDonald brothers were in that range. But let's also say that leadership isn't even on your radar. You don't care about it, and you make no effort to develop as a leader. You're functioning as a 1. Your level of effectiveness would look like this:

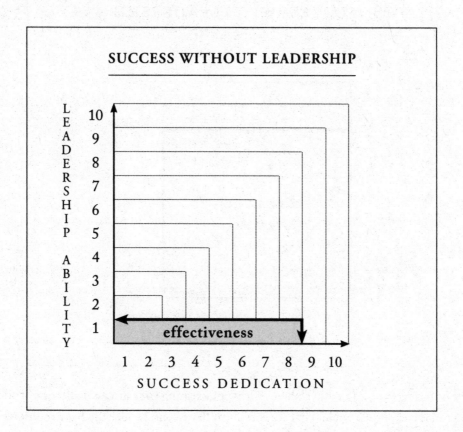

To increase your level of effectiveness, you have a couple of choices. You could work very hard to increase your dedication to success and excellence—to work toward becoming a 10. It's possible that you could make it to that level, though the Law of Diminishing Returns says that the effort it would take to increase those last two points might take more energy than it did to achieve the first eight. If you really killed yourself, you might increase your success by that 25 percent.

But you have another option. You can work hard to increase your level of *leadership*. Let's say that your natural leadership ability is a 4—slightly below average. Just by using whatever natural talent you have, you already increase your effectiveness fourfold. But let's say you become a real student of leadership and you maximize your potential. You take it all the way up to a 7. Visually, the results would look like this:

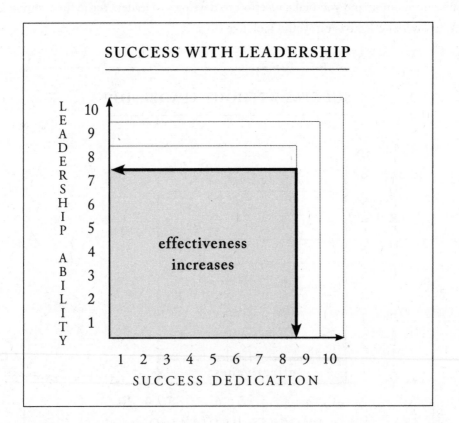

By raising your leadership ability—without increasing your success dedication at all—you can increase your original effectiveness by 600 percent. Leadership has a multiplying effect.

DISCUSS

Answer the following questions and discuss your answers when you meet with your team.

1 How effective will people be if they increase their leadership but not their work ethic (dedication to success)?

_____

_____

_____

_____

2 Do you agree with the statement that increasing your leadership is one of the best ways to increase your level of effectiveness? Explain.

_____

_____

_____

_____

3 What criteria can be used to determine a person's leadership ability? What are some clear signs of leadership strengths and weaknesses?

_____

_____

_____

_____

4 How long does it take you to determine a person's leadership "lid" once that person has been put in charge of a team?

_____

_____

_____

_____

5 What are some signs that indicate a leader has hit his or her lid?

_____

_____

_____

_____

_____

_____

6 When has your leadership lid negatively affected a project or task?

_____

_____

_____

_____

_____

_____

7 On a scale of 1 to 10, how would you describe your leadership? Would your spouse or colleagues agree with your assessment?

_____

_____

_____

_____

_____

_____

8 Up to now, how dedicated have you been to developing yourself as a leader? How will you increase that dedication?

_____

_____

_____

_____

_____

_____

APPLY

1 List some of your major goals. (Try to focus on significant objectives—things that will require a year or longer of your time. List at least five but no more than ten items.) Now identify which ones will require the participation or cooperation of other people. For these activities, your leadership ability will greatly impact your effectiveness.

_____

_____

_____

_____

_____

2 Assess your leadership ability. Review the leadership assessment you took at the start of this workbook to get an idea of your basic leadership ability.

_____

_____

_____

_____

3 Ask others to rate your leadership. Talk to your boss, your spouse, two colleagues (at your level), and three people you lead about your leadership ability. Ask each of them to rate you on a scale of 1 (low) to 10 (high) in each of the following areas:

- People skills
- Planning and strategic thinking
- Vision
- Results

_____

_____

_____

_____

_____

Average the scores and compare them to your own assessment. Based on these assessments, is your leadership skill better or worse than you expected? If there is a gap between your assessment and that of others, what do you think is the cause? How willing are you to grow in the area of leadership?

TAKE ACTION

Interview someone whom you consider to have a high leadership lid. Ideally, this would be the person you listed in the OBSERVE section for "someone you know whose leadership lid seems unlimited." Ask that person the following questions:

1 When did you first see yourself as a leader?

_____
_____
_____
_____
_____

2 What are some of the greatest challenges you've faced as a leader?

_____
_____
_____
_____
_____

3 What has contributed to your growth as a leader?

_____
_____
_____
_____

4 What are you currently doing to grow as a leader?

_____

_____

_____

_____

5 What is the best piece of advice that you would have for someone who aspires to be an effective leader?

_____

_____

_____

_____

2

---◆◆◆---

THE LAW OF INFLUENCE

The True Measure of Leadership Is Influence—Nothing More, Nothing Less

If you don't have influence, you will *never* be able to lead others. As psychologist Harry A. Overstreet observed, "The very essence of all power to influence lies in getting the other person to participate."[1] If no one is following you, you're not a leader. The Law of Influence is about obtaining followers, which makes it the basis for leadership.

READ

One of my favorite stories that illustrates the Law of Influence concerns Abraham Lincoln. In 1832, decades before he became president, young Lincoln gathered together a group of men to fight in the Black Hawk War. In those days, the person who put together a volunteer company for the militia often became its leader and assumed a commanding rank. In this instance, Lincoln was given the rank of captain. But Lincoln had a problem. He knew nothing about soldiering. He had no prior military experience, and he knew nothing about tactics. He had trouble remembering the simplest military procedures.

For example, one day Lincoln was marching a couple of dozen men across a field and needed to guide them through a gate into another field. But he couldn't manage it. Recounting the incident later, Lincoln said, "I could not for the life of me remember the proper word of command for getting my company endwise. Finally, as we came near [the

13

gate] I shouted: 'This company is dismissed for two minutes, when it will fall in again on the other side of the gate.'"[2]

As time went by, Lincoln's level of influence with others in the militia actually *decreased*. While other officers proved themselves and gained rank, Lincoln found himself going in the other direction. He began as a captain, but *title and position* did him little good. He couldn't overcome the Law of Influence. By the end of his military service, Abraham Lincoln had found his rightful place, having achieved the rank of private.

Fortunately for Lincoln—and for the fate of the United States—he overcame his inability to influence others. Lincoln followed his time in the military with undistinguished stints in the Illinois state legislature and the U.S. House of Representatives. But over time and with much effort and personal experience, he became a person of remarkable influence and impact, and one of the nation's finest presidents.

I love the leadership proverb that says, "He who thinks he leads, but has no followers, is only taking a walk." If you can't influence people, then they will not follow you. And if people won't follow, you are not a leader. That's the Law of Influence. No matter what anybody else may tell you, remember that leadership is influence—nothing more, nothing less.

OBSERVE

Leadership is often misunderstood. When people hear that someone has an impressive title or an assigned leadership position, they assume that individual to be a leader. Sometimes that's true. But titles don't have much value when it comes to leading. True leadership cannot be awarded, appointed, or assigned. It comes only from influence, and that cannot be mandated. It must be earned. The only thing a title can buy is a little time—either to increase your level of influence with others or to undermine it.

1 Why was Lincoln an ineffective captain?

_____

_____

_____

_____

_____

2 How did Lincoln's inability to influence others affect his military career?

_____

_____

_____

_____

_____

3 What is the most basic factor you can use to determine if someone is a leader or not?

_____

_____

_____

_____

_____

4 According to the definition "leadership is influence," who are the most prominent leaders in your industry? What influence do they have over industry trends and standards?

_____

_____

_____

_____

_____

5 Within your organization, who is not formally recognized as a leader but has influence with others?

_____

_____

_____

_____

_____

LEARN

Through the years, I've encountered many other misconceptions and myths people embrace about leaders and leadership. I want to share with you five common ones:

1. The Management Myth

A widespread misunderstanding is that leading and managing are one and the same. Up until a few decades ago, books that claimed to be on leadership were often really about management. The main difference between the two is that leadership is about influencing people to follow, while management focuses on maintaining systems and processes. As former Chrysler chairman and CEO Lee Iacocca wryly commented, "Sometimes even the best manager is like the little boy with the big dog, waiting to see where the dog wants to go so that he can take him there."

The best way to test whether a person can lead rather than just manage is to ask him to create positive change. Managers can maintain direction, but often they can't change it. Systems and processes can do only so much. To move people in a new direction, you need influence.

2. The Entrepreneur Myth

Frequently, people assume that all entrepreneurs are leaders. But that's not always the case. Entrepreneurs are skilled at seeing opportunities and going after them. They see needs and understand how to meet them in a way that produces a profit. But not all entrepreneurs are good with people. Many find it necessary to partner with someone skilled at the people part of the equation. If they can't influence people, they can't lead.

3. The Knowledge Myth

Sir Francis Bacon said, "Knowledge is power." If you believe power to be the essence of leadership, then you might naturally assume that those who possess knowledge and intelligence are therefore leaders. That isn't necessarily true. You can visit any major university and meet brilliant research scientists and philosophers whose ability to think is so high that it's off the charts, but whose ability to lead is so low that it doesn't even register *on* the charts. Neither IQ nor education necessarily equates to leadership.

4. THE PIONEER MYTH

Another misconception is that anyone who is out in front of the crowd is a leader. But being first isn't always the same as leading. For example, Sir Edmund Hillary was the first man to reach the summit of Mount Everest. Since his historic ascent in 1953, hundreds of people have "followed" him in achieving that feat. But that doesn't make Hillary a leader. He wasn't even the official leader on the expedition when he reached the summit. John Hunt was. And when Hillary traveled to the South Pole in 1958 as part of the Commonwealth Trans-Antarctic Expedition, he was accompanying another leader, Sir Vivian Fuchs. To be a leader, a person has to not only be out front, but also have people intentionally coming behind him, following his lead, and acting on his vision. Being a trendsetter is not the same as being a leader.

5. THE POSITION MYTH

As mentioned earlier, the greatest misunderstanding about leadership is thinking it is based primarily on position. It's not. If you've ever declined to follow a bad boss, or if you've ever been appointed to a position on a team or committee and people didn't listen to your advice or take your direction, you know that a title doesn't make you a leader. A position only gives you a chance. Stanley Huffty affirmed, "It's not the position that makes the leader; it's the leader that makes the position."

Although people in your organization may buy into one of these myths, when all is said and done, true leadership is *influence*. Leadership is the ability to obtain followers. It is the ability to influence others to follow you. Because without followers, who are you leading?

DISCUSS

Answer the following questions and discuss your answers when you meet with your team.

1 What is the difference between management and leadership?

_____

_____

_____

_____

2 Do you agree with the statement that "leadership is influence"? Explain.

_____

_____

_____

_____

_____

3 What obstacles might people come up against if they have bought into one of the leadership myths?

_____

_____

_____

_____

4 When have you been part of a team that was led by a person who was placed in charge because of his or her knowledge or position and not his or her leadership abilities?

_____

_____

_____

_____

_____

5 Would you consider yourself to be a leader? Whom do you influence?

_____

_____

_____

_____

6 What are some positive ways you could expand your influence in your organization?

_____

_____

_____

_____

APPLY

1 Which of the myths in this lesson have you bought into in the past: management, entrepreneur, knowledge, pioneer, or position? Why have you been susceptible to that myth? What does that say about your perception of leadership up until now? What must you change in your current thinking to make you more open to improving your leadership in the future?

_____

_____

_____

_____

2 What do you usually rely upon most to persuade people to follow you? Rate yourself on a scale of 1 to 10 for each of the following factors (a score of 1 means it's not a factor, while a score of 10 means you rely on it continually):

____ Character—who you are

____ Relationships—who you know

____ Knowledge—what you know

____ Intuition—what you feel

____ Experience—where you've been

____ Past success—what you've done

____ Ability—what you can do

How can you optimize or better utilize the ones with low scores?

3 Find an organization for a cause you believe in and volunteer. If you believe you have leadership ability, then after building relationships, try leading. It will help you learn to lead through influence.

_____

_____

_____

_____

_____

TAKE ACTION

This week, try to influence five people: a supervisor, a colleague on your same position level, a follower in your sphere of influence, a follower outside of your sphere of influence, and a family member or close friend. It could be as simple as suggesting where to go eat, or as critical as suggesting a new direction for a project. At the end of the week, review each situation by following the instructions noted.

SUPERIOR: _____

My expectation:

_____

_____

_____

_____

Result and explanation:

_____

_____

_____

_____

COLLEAGUE—ON SAME POSITION LEVEL: _____

My expectation:

_____

_____

_____

_____

Result and explanation:

_____

_____

_____

_____

FOLLOWER—IN YOUR AREA OF INFLUENCE: _____

My expectation:

_____

_____

_____

_____

Result and explanation:

_____

_____

_____

_____

FOLLOWER—NOT IN YOUR AREA OF INFLUENCE: _____

My expectation:

_____

_____

_____

Result and explanation:

_____

_____

_____

FAMILY MEMBER OR CLOSE FRIEND: _____

My expectation: **Result and explanation:**

_____   _____

_____   _____

_____   _____

_____   _____

In what instances were you successful in influencing others to go along with your idea? Put a (+) next to these occurrences.

In what instances were you unsuccessful in influencing others to go along with your idea? Put a (✓) next to these occurrences.

For each situation, evaluate why you expected someone to follow your lead. Was it because you were in a position of authority? Or you were the most knowledgeable person on the subject? Or you were the person who came up with the original idea? Or you were the recognized leader? Evaluate why you think people did or did not follow your lead.

1 When do you find yourself being influenced by someone else because of his or her position, knowledge, or leadership?

_____

_____

_____

_____

2 How is that similar to the way people have responded to you?

_____

_____

_____

_____

3

THE LAW OF PROCESS

Leadership Develops Daily, Not in a Day

Becoming a leader is a lot like investing successfully in the stock market. If your hope is to make a fortune in a day, you're not going to be successful. There are no successful "day traders" in leadership development. What matters most is what you do day by day over the long haul.

READ

There is an old saying: champions don't become champions in the ring—they are merely recognized there. That's true. If you want to see where someone develops into a champion, look at his daily routine. Former heavyweight champ Joe Frazier stated, "You can map out a fight plan or a life plan. But when the action starts, you're down to your reflexes. That's where your road work shows. If you cheated on that in the dark of the morning, you're getting found out now under the bright lights."[1] Boxing is a good analogy for leadership development because it is all about daily preparation. Even a person with natural talent has to prepare and train to become successful.

One of this country's greatest leaders was a fan of boxing: President Theodore Roosevelt. In fact, one of his most famous quotes uses a boxing analogy:

It is not the critic who counts, not the man who points out how the strong man stumbled, or where the doer of deeds could have done them better. The credit belongs to the man who is actually in the arena; whose face is marred by dust and sweat and blood;

who strives valiantly; who errs and comes short again and again; who knows the great enthusiasms, the great devotions, and spends himself in a worthy cause; who, at best, knows in the end the triumph of high achievement; and who, at the worst, if he fails, at least fails while daring greatly, so that his place shall never be with those cold and timid souls who know neither victory nor defeat.[2]

Roosevelt, a boxer himself, was the ultimate man of action. Not only was he an effective leader, but he was one of the most flamboyant of all US presidents. British historian Hugh Brogan described him as "the ablest man to sit in the White House since Lincoln; the most vigorous since Jackson; the most bookish since John Quincy Adams."

TR (Roosevelt's nickname) is remembered as an outspoken man of action and proponent of the vigorous life. While in the White House, he was known for regular boxing and judo sessions, challenging horseback rides, and long, strenuous hikes. A French ambassador who visited Roosevelt used to tell about the time that he accompanied the president on a walk through the woods. When the two men came to the banks of a stream that was too deep to cross by foot, TR stripped off his clothes and expected the dignitary to do the same so that they could swim to the other side. Nothing was an obstacle to Roosevelt.

At different times in his life, Roosevelt was a cowboy in the Wild West, an explorer and big-game hunter, and a roughriding cavalry officer in the Spanish-American War. His enthusiasm and stamina seemed boundless. As the vice-presidential candidate in 1900, he gave 673 speeches and traveled 20,000 miles while campaigning for President McKinley. And years after his presidency, while preparing to deliver a speech in Milwaukee, Roosevelt was shot by a would-be assassin. With a broken rib and a bullet in his chest, Roosevelt insisted on delivering his one-hour speech before allowing himself to be taken to the hospital.

Of all the leaders this nation has ever had, Roosevelt was one of the toughest—both physically and mentally. But he didn't start that way. America's cowboy president was born in Manhattan to a prominent wealthy family. As a child, he was puny and sickly. He had debilitating asthma, possessed very poor eyesight, and was painfully thin. His parents weren't sure he would survive.

When he was twelve, young Roosevelt's father told him, "You have the mind, but you have not the body, and without the help of the body the mind cannot go as far as it should. You must *make* the body." Make it he did. He lived by the Law of Process.

TR began spending time *every day* building his body as well as his mind, and he did that for the rest of his life. He worked out with weights, hiked, ice-skated, hunted, rowed, rode horseback, and boxed. Roosevelt said, "I had a great admiration for men who were fearless and who could hold their own in the world, and I had a great desire to be like them." By the time TR graduated from Harvard, he *was* like them, and he was ready to tackle the world of politics.

Roosevelt didn't become a great leader overnight, either. His road to the presidency was one of slow, continual growth. As he served in various positions, ranging from New York City police commissioner to president of the United States, he kept learning and growing, and in time he became a strong leader. Under his leadership, the United States emerged as a world power, developed a first-class navy, and built the Panama Canal. He negotiated peace between Russia and Japan, winning a Nobel Peace Prize in the process. And when people questioned TR's leadership—he had first become president when McKinley was assassinated—he campaigned and was reelected by the largest majority of any president up to his time.

On January 6, 1919, at his home in New York, Theodore Roosevelt died in his sleep. Then Vice President Marshall said, "Death had to take him sleeping, for if Roosevelt had been awake, there would have been a fight." When they removed him from his bed, they found a book under his pillow. Up to the very last, TR was still striving to learn and improve himself. He was still practicing the Law of Process.

If you want to be a leader, the good news is that you can do it. Everyone has the potential, but it isn't accomplished overnight. It requires perseverance. And you absolutely cannot ignore the Law of Process. Leadership doesn't develop in a day. It takes a lifetime.

OBSERVE

My friend Tag Short maintains, "The secret of our success is found in our daily agenda." If you continually invest in your leadership development, letting your "assets" compound, the inevitable result is growth over time.

1 What are some of the challenges that Roosevelt had to overcome in order to become a great leader?

_____

_____

_____

_____

2 What are some things that Roosevelt included in his daily agenda that contributed to his leadership ability?

_____

_____

_____

_____

3 Roosevelt looked to his father and other leaders that he read about for inspiration. Who are some of the people you look to for inspiration? Why?

_____

_____

_____

_____

4 Whom do you admire in your profession or area of service? Why is this person inspirational?

_____

_____

_____

_____

5 Who in your profession or area of service do you think could have achieved more than he or she did? Why do you think this person settled for less? How does this person's dedication to personal growth factor into his or her level of success?

_____

_____

_____

_____

6 Which person from questions 4 and 5 do you more identify with? Why?

_____

_____

_____

_____

LEARN

LEADERSHIP IS LIKE INVESTING—IT COMPOUNDS

Becoming a leader is a lot like investing successfully in the stock market. If your hope is to make a fortune in a day, you're not likely to be successful. There are no successful "day traders" in leadership development. What matters most is what you do day by day over the long haul. My friend Tag Short maintains, "The secret of our success is found in our daily agenda." If you continually invest in your leadership development, letting your "assets" compound, the inevitable result is growth over time. What can you see when you look at a person's daily agenda? Priorities, passion, abilities, relationships, attitude, personal disciplines, vision, and influence. See what a person is doing every day, day after day, and you'll know who that person is and what he or she is becoming.

When I teach leadership at conferences, people inevitably ask me if leaders are born. I always answer, "Yes, of course they are . . . I've yet to meet an unborn leader! How else would you expect them to come into the world?" We all laugh, and then I answer the real question—whether leadership is something a person either is born with and possesses or is not born with and doesn't. I can tell you: leadership can be learned.

If a genie appeared and gave me just one wish, it would be that people who learn leadership from me now could have seen me fifty years ago. I was not a good leader because I truly did not understand it. In my first leadership position, I led through popularity. I was charismatic and energetic, and I could make things fun. So people joined along with me. But I didn't really take anyone anywhere. And when I left the organization, it collapsed because I had gathered a crowd, but when I left, the crowd dispersed.

I spent probably six months trying to figure out what happened and where I went wrong. At the end of that time, I came to the conclusion that I was trying to lead out of personality instead of a process. That's a problem because personality always takes shortcuts. I wanted people to like me, but I wasn't doing anything to help them change their behavior, take action, and win. Good leadership is bigger and better than one person.

You may have been born with many great natural gifts or few. That's not important in the end, because the ability to lead is really a collection of skills, nearly all of which can be learned and improved. If you have loads of talent but never develop it, you will not lead as well as people with fewer gifts who dedicate themselves to the Law of Process.

Becoming a better leader is a process that doesn't happen overnight. Leadership is complicated. It has many facets: respect, experience, emotional strength, people skills, discipline, vision, momentum, timing—the list goes on. As you can see, many factors that come into play in leadership are intangible. That's why leaders require so much seasoning to be effective.

LEADERS ARE LEARNERS

In a study of ninety top leaders from a variety of fields, leadership experts Warren Bennis and Burt Nanus made a discovery about the relationship between growth and leadership: "It is the capacity to develop and improve their skills that distinguishes leaders from their followers." Successful leaders are learners. And the learning process is ongoing, a result of self-discipline and perseverance. The goal each day must be to get a little better, to build on the previous day's progress.

The problem is that most people overestimate the importance of events and underestimate the power of processes. We want quick fixes. We want the compounding effect that Anne Scheiber received over fifty years, but we want it in fifty minutes.

Don't get me wrong. I appreciate events. They can be effective catalysts. But if you want lasting improvement, if you want power, then rely on a process. Consider the difference between the two:

An Event	A Process
Encourages decisions	Encourages development
Motivates people	Matures people
Is a calendar issue	Is a culture issue
Challenges people	Changes people
Is easy	Is difficult

If I need to be inspired to take steps forward, then I'll attend an event. If I want to improve, then I'll engage in a process and stick with it.

CONSISTENCY COMPOUNDS

As a young leader, I discovered the Law of Process when I learned that I had to keep growing if I wanted to become a good leader. More than fifty years have gone by since then, and what I've discovered is that consistency compounds. By working to grow a little every day, I've grown a lot over the years. It takes time for the little things to add up to big things. Too often, we get discouraged because we don't see great leaps in our growth. What we need to remember is that most changes occur gradually. It's like trying to freeze room temperature water. If you put water outside on a cold winter day, it will start changing from 75 degrees Fahrenheit, down to 74, 73, 72, but it looks like nothing is happening. The water temperature goes down into the sixties, fifties, then forties. Still it looks like nothing's happening. It keeps dropping: 38, 37, 36, 35, 34, 33. So much time has gone by that you're ready to give up. Then it drops down to 32 and a major change occurs. It's a breakthrough change.

Leaders are the same way. They need to keep learning and growing, even if they don't see the payoff. Sometimes we are so close to having a compounding victory and we don't know it. If we give up before the change, we miss it. Persistence pays. Consistency compounds. As martial arts legend Bruce Lee said, "Long term consistency trumps short term intensity."

Leadership is developed daily, not in a day. That is the reality dictated by the Law of Process. Benjamin Disraeli asserted, "The secret of success in life is for a man to be ready for his time when it comes." What a person does on a disciplined, consistent basis gets him ready, no matter what the goal.

DISCUSS

Answer the following questions and discuss your answers when you meet with your team.

1 According to the Law of Process, to what must you be committed in order to become a successful leader?

_____

_____

_____

_____

2 Do you agree with the statement that leadership is a process? Why or why not?

_____

_____

_____

_____

3 Is leadership only for a few people? Why?

_____

_____

_____

_____

_____

_____

4 How are you investing in yourself to become a better leader?

_____

_____

_____

_____

_____

_____

5 How are you investing in yourself daily to become a better leader?

_____

_____

_____

_____

_____

_____

6 In the last year, what has contributed the most to your growth as a leader?

_____

_____

_____

_____

APPLY

1   How will you intentionally grow as a leader? Do you have a plan? If not, write one out. I recommend that you read one book a month, listen to at least one message or podcast a week, and attend one conference a year. Select the materials in advance, put time for growth on your calendar, and start immediately. If developing a plan from scratch seems difficult, you may want to read my book *Today Matters*. That contains the personal growth plan I have used for years.

_____

_____

_____

_____

2   One thing that separates great leaders from good leaders is the way they invest in those who follow them. Just as you need a growth plan to improve, so do those who work for you. You can take groups of employees through books, bring in trainers, mentor people one on one—anything that works. Make providing opportunities for growth your responsibility.

_____

_____

_____

_____

3   If you are the leader of a business, an organization, or a department, you can create a culture of growth. When people in your sphere of influence know that personal growth and leadership development are valued, resourced, and rewarded, then growth will explode. And the environment you create will begin attracting high achievers and people with great potential.

_____

_____

_____

_____

TAKE ACTION

While it is true that some people are born with greater natural gifts than others, the ability to lead is really a collection of skills, nearly all of which can be learned and improved. But that process doesn't happen overnight. Leadership is complicated. It has many facets: respect, experience, emotional strength, people skills, discipline, vision, momentum, timing—the list goes on. As you can see, many factors that come into play in leadership are intangible. That's why leaders require so much seasoning to be effective.

This week, research or interview the person you admire as a leader in your profession or area of service. Ask that person the following questions.

1. What made you decide to enter the field in which you are successful?
2. Who were some of your mentors?
3. What five books have made the greatest impact on your leadership?
4. What daily learning or self-improvement habits do you have?

Ask yourself: *What are the three most valuable things I have learned from this person's life that I can apply to my own leadership growth?* Start reading one of the five books recommended to you.

4

◆◆◆

THE LAW OF NAVIGATION

Anyone Can Steer the Ship, but It
Takes a Leader to Chart the Course

One thing all leaders have in common is the ability to see more and before—they see more than others do because they see the big picture, and they see what's coming before others do. This gives them an advantage when it comes to navigating for the people they lead. In order to be a successful leader, you must learn the importance of The Law of Navigation and be willing to navigate the course for your followers.

READ

In 1911, two groups of explorers set off on an incredible mission. Though they used different strategies and routes, the leaders of the teams had the same goal: to be the first in history to reach the South Pole. Their stories are life-and-death illustrations of the Law of Navigation.

One group was led by Norwegian explorer Roald Amundsen. Ironically, Amundsen had not originally intended to go to Antarctica. His desire was to be the first man to reach the North Pole. But when he learned that Robert Peary had beaten him there, Amundsen changed his goal and headed toward the other end of the earth. North or south—he knew his planning would pay off.

Before his team ever set off, Amundsen had assessed the coming challenges and painstakingly planned his trip. He studied the methods of the indigenous Arctic people and other experienced cold-weather travelers, and he determined that their best course of action would be to transport all their equipment and supplies by dogsled. When he assembled his team, he chose expert skiers and dog handlers. His strategy was simple. The dogs would do most of the work as the group traveled fifteen to twenty miles in a six-hour period each day. That would afford both the dogs and the men plenty of time for daily rest prior to the following day's travel.

Amundsen's forethought and attention to detail were incredible. He located and stocked supply depots all along the intended route. That way they would not have to carry every bit of their supplies with them the whole trip. He also equipped his people with the best gear possible. Before he set off, Amundsen had taken the trip in his mind, carefully considering every possible aspect of the journey, thinking it through, and planning accordingly. And it paid off. The worst problem they experienced on their trip was an infected tooth one man needed to have extracted.

The other team of people was led by Robert Falcon Scott, a British naval officer who had previously done some exploring in the Antarctic area. Scott's expedition was the antithesis of Amundsen's. Instead of using dogsleds, Scott decided to use motorized sledges and ponies. Their problems began when the motors on the sledges stopped working only five days into the trip. The ponies didn't fare well either in those frigid temperatures. When they reached the foot of the Transantarctic Mountains, all of the poor animals had to be killed. As a result, the team members themselves ended up hauling the two-hundred-pound sledges. It was arduous work.

Scott hadn't given enough attention to the team's other equipment either. Everyone on the team developed frostbite and became snow-blind because of inadequate clothing and goggles. The team was always low on food and water. The depots of supplies were inadequately stocked, too far apart, and poorly marked, making them very difficult to find. Because they were continually low on fuel to melt snow, everyone became dehydrated. Making things even worse was Scott's last-minute decision to take along a fifth man, even though they had prepared enough supplies for only four.

After covering a grueling eight hundred miles in ten weeks, Scott's exhausted group finally arrived at the South Pole on January 17, 1912. There they found the Norwegian flag flapping in the wind and a letter from Amundsen. The other well-led team had beaten them there by more than a month!

Scott's expedition to the South Pole is a classic example of a leader who could not navigate for his people. But their trek back was even worse. Scott insisted that they collect and carry back thirty pounds of geological specimens—more weight to be carried by the worn-out men. The group's progress became slower and slower. One member of the party sank into a stupor and died. Another, suffering severe frostbite, purposely walked out into a blizzard to keep from hindering the group. Before he left the tent, he said, "I am just going outside; I may be some time."

Scott and his final two team members made it only a little farther north before giving up. They died 150 miles from their base camp. We know their story only because they spent their last hours updating their diaries and writing letters.

Some of the last words Scott wrote were: "We have been to the Pole and we shall die like gentlemen. . . . I think this will show that the spirit of pluck and power to endure has not passed out of our race. . . . We very nearly came through and it's a pity to have missed it, but lately I have felt that we have overshot the mark."[1] Scott had great courage. But only at the end did he recognize his shortcomings. Finally he saw that anyone can steer the ship, but it takes a leader to chart the course. Because he did not live by the Law of Navigation, he and his companions died by it.

OBSERVE

Followers need leaders able to effectively navigate for them. When they're facing life-and-death situations, the necessity is painfully obvious. But even when consequences aren't as serious, the need is also great. The truth is that nearly anyone can *steer* the ship, but it takes a leader to chart the course.

1 What are some of the things that Amundsen planned for that Scott overlooked?

_____

_____

_____

_____

2 How did Scott's lack of leadership skills affect his team?

_____

_____

_____

_____

3　In your organization, what events or projects could have been planned better? What would the outcome have been if the team had a leader who was a good navigator?

_____

_____

_____

_____

4　Who are the top navigators in your field? How have their leadership skills benefited their organizations?

_____

_____

_____

_____

LEARN

First-rate navigators always have in mind that people are depending on them and their ability to chart a good course. I read an observation by James A. Autry in *Life and Work: A Manager's Search for Meaning* that illustrates this idea. He wrote that occasionally you hear about the crash of four military planes flying together in a formation. The reason for the loss of all four is this: when jet fighters fly in groups of four, one pilot—the leader—designates where the team will fly. The other three planes fly on the leader's wing, adjusting to him and following wherever he goes. Whatever moves the leader makes, the rest of the team will make along with him. That's true whether he soars in the clouds or smashes into a mountaintop.[2]

Before good leaders take their people on a journey, they take steps to give the trip the best chance for success:

1. NAVIGATORS KEEP THEIR EMOTIONS FROM CLOUDING THEIR VISION

No matter the conditions leaders face, they must not panic. They can't let the circumstances prevent them from seeing more and before and from navigating people through their difficulties. Tom Morris, in his book *Plato's Lemonade Stand*, offers a metaphor that can help leaders avoid getting caught up in emotion that might otherwise paralyze them:

> Imagine life as a large wagon wheel. If we emotionally live on the outer rim, then as the wheel turns, we'll be spun around to extreme highs and lows in rapid and dizzying succession. But if we can learn to move closer in toward the mid point of the hub, we become much more centered. The wheel will still spin, but we won't be so dramatically thrown by its motion. That's a position of power.[3]

The best navigators are able to delay their emotions long enough to work through a problem when people are depending on them to lead. How can they do that? First, by knowing and staying true to their definition of success. For example, the definition of success that guides me internally states that success is having those closest to me love and respect me the most. This keeps me grounded and faithful. My external definition of success is knowing my purpose, growing to my potential, and sowing seeds that benefit others. These two definitions give me perspective as I face challenges.

The second factor that helps good navigators keep their heads in the midst of difficult circumstances is dedication to being bigger on the inside than the outside. This comes from having more faith than fear and from embracing good values. When facing difficult times, values keep us from losing our way or giving up.

2. Navigators Draw on Past Experience

Every past success and failure you've experienced can be a valuable source of information and wisdom—if you allow it to be. While successes can teach you what you're capable of doing and gives you confidence, failures often teach greater lessons. They reveal wrong assumptions, character flaws, errors in judgment, and poor working methods. Ironically, many people hate their failures so much that they quickly cover them up instead of analyzing them and learning from them. As I explain in my book *Failing Forward*, if you fail to learn from your mistakes, you're going to fail again and again.

Why do I even mention something that seems so basic? Because most natural leaders are activists. They tend to look forward (not backward), make decisions, and move on. I know this because that is my tendency. But I'm not very good at navigating. It's one of my leadership weaknesses. Good navigators take time to reflect and learn from their experiences. I wrote about this in my book *How Successful People Think*, but allow me to recount some advantages of reflective thinking here. Reflective thinking . . .

- Gives you true perspective.
- Gives emotional integrity to your thought life.
- Increases your confidence in decision making.
- Clarifies the big picture.
- Takes a good experience and makes it a valuable experience.

Each benefit gives a leader a great advantage when planning next steps for a team or organization.

3. Navigators Examine the Conditions Before Committing

Drawing on experience means looking inward. Examining conditions means looking outward. No good leader plans a course of action without paying close attention to current conditions. That would be like setting sail against the tide or plotting a course into a hurricane. Good navigators look at the present and try to anticipate the future so that they can count the cost *before* making commitments for themselves and their team. They examine not only measurable factors such as finances, resources, and talent, but also intangibles such as timing, morale, momentum, culture, and so on. (I'll discuss this more in the Laws of Intuition and Timing.)

4. Navigators Listen to Others

No matter how much you learn from the past, it will never tell you all that you need to know about the present. No matter how good a leader you are, you will not see everything you need to. That's why top-notch navigators gather information from many sources. For example, before Roald Amundsen's expedition to the South Pole, he learned from a group of Native Americans in Canada about warm clothing and Arctic survival techniques. Those skills and practices meant the difference between failure and success for his team in Antarctica.

Navigating leaders get ideas from many sources. They listen to members of their leadership team. They talk to the people in their organization to find out what's happening at the grassroots level. And they spend time with leaders from outside the organization who can mentor them. They always think in terms of relying on a team, not just themselves.

5. NAVIGATORS BALANCE BOTH FAITH AND FACT

Being able to navigate for others requires a leader to possess a positive attitude. You've got to have faith that you can take your people all the way. If you can't confidently make the trip in your mind, you're not going to be able to take it in real life.

On the other hand, you also have to be able to realistically deal with facts. You can't minimize obstacles or rationalize challenges and still navigate effectively. Pretending obstacles don't exist won't help you to overcome them. If you don't go in with your eyes wide open, you're going to get blindsided.

Jim Collins confirmed this balance between faith and fact in his 2001 book *Good to Great*. He calls it the Stockdale Paradox, after Admiral Jim Stockdale, and writes, "You must retain faith that you will prevail in the end *and* you must also confront the most brutal facts of your current reality." Balancing optimism and realism, intuition and planning, faith and fact can be very difficult. But that's what it takes to be effective as a navigating leader.

DISCUSS

Answer the following questions and discuss your answers when you meet with your team.

1 What is the process you should go through in order to successfully navigate your team?

_____

_____

_____

_____

_____

2 Do you agree that all five steps in the navigation process are necessary? Explain.

_____

_____

_____

_____

_____

3 | Which step in the navigation process do you find most difficult? Why?

_____

_____

_____

_____

_____

4 | How do you choose who to run your ideas by before implementing them?

_____

_____

_____

_____

_____

5 | Think of a time when you skipped one of the steps in the navigation process. What was the outcome?

_____

_____

_____

_____

_____

6 | How do you prepare your team for projects? Do you need to spend more time on planning? What prevents you from doing so? How can you more effectively plan to plan?

_____

_____

_____

_____

_____

APPLY

1 Do you make it a regular practice to reflect on your positive and negative experiences? If not, you will miss the potential lessons they have to offer. Do one of two things. Set aside a time to reflect every week, examining your calendar or journal to jog your memory. Or build reflection time into your schedule, so that it's immediately available after every major success or failure. In either case, write down what you learn during that discovery process.

_____

_____

_____

_____

2 Leaders who navigate well do their homework. For a current project or objective, draw on your past experience, have intentional conversations with experts and team members to gather information, and examine current conditions to inform your navigational planning. Once you've taken these steps, and formed your action plan, take action.

_____

_____

_____

3 Which way do you naturally lean—toward faith or facts? Are you highly visionary and optimistic, believing that anything is possible? Or do you focus on facts without giving much attention to intangibles? To successfully practice the Law of Navigation, you must embrace both. Enlist opposite-thinking people on your team to help you. Work together to navigate to success.

_____

_____

_____

_____

TAKE ACTION

Use the following acrostic based on *Plan Ahead* to execute an upcoming project with your team. Follow the example given.

EXAMPLE PROJECT: COMPANY GROWTH

*P*redetermine a course of action

> In order to grow, we need a new facility.

*L*ay out your goals

> Our goals are to design the facility, build the facility, pay for it in ten years, and keep morale high in the process.

*A*djust your priorities

> Our priority is to have a solid financial plan so the business isn't strained during the building process.

*N*otify key personnel

> The people who need to know about the plan are those with the most influence, key leaders, people working on the project.

*A*llow time for acceptance

> We will announce the project in two-hour presentations to the board and follow up three days later.

*H*ead into action

> The first step for building the new facility is zoning.

*E*xpect problems

> A roadblock to our progress may be zoning issues. We will plan for this roadblock by researching the zoning laws in our county.

*A*lways point to successes

> We will give success updates by sending out a memo every other Monday morning.

*D*aily review your planning

> The project leaders will communicate each day by holding a fifteen-minute meeting each morning.

5

THE LAW OF ADDITION

Leaders Add Value by Serving Others

Many people view leadership the same way they view success, hoping to go as far as they can, to climb the ladder, to achieve the highest position possible for someone with their talent. But contrary to conventional thinking, I believe the bottom line in leadership isn't how far we advance ourselves but how far we advance others. That is achieved by serving others and adding value to their lives.

READ

In a world where many political leaders enjoy their power and prestige and where CEOs of large corporations make astronomical incomes, work and live in luxury, and appear to be most concerned with what's in it for them, Jim Sinegal was an oddity.

Sinegal is the cofounder and former CEO of Costco, one of the largest retailers in the world and an organization that regularly ranks near the top as a best brand, admired company, and respected retailer.[1] He retired in 2012. While he was CEO, Sinegal didn't seem much interested in the perks of leadership. He worked in an unremarkable office comprised primarily of folding tables and chairs. If he invited people to meet him at the corporate offices, he went down to the lobby himself to meet them. He answered his own phone. And the salary he took was modest: a third of the average CEO's salary during his tenure.[2]

Sinegal's path to corporate leadership wasn't typical either. He didn't attend an Ivy League school. He wasn't a lawyer or a CPA. As a teenager, he thought of becoming a doctor, but his high school grades were less than stellar. So he went off to community college and earned an associate degree. While he was attending San Diego State College (now University), he helped a friend unload mattresses at a new local retail store called Fed-Mart. What he expected to be one day of work turned into a regular job. When he received a promotion, he discontinued his studies. He had found his career and a mentor, Sol Price, Fed-Mart's chairman. Under Price's guidance, Sinegal rose to the post of executive vice president for merchandising. Sinegal later helped Price found Price Club, then went on to cofound Costco in 1983 with Jeffrey H. Brotman. The company's growth was rapid. Costco purchased and merged with Price Club ten years later.

Retail experts give a lot of attention to Sinegal's formula for success: offer a limited number of items, rely on high volume sales, keep costs as low as possible, and don't spend money on advertising. But there is something that separated him from the competitors who employ similar strategies: the way he treated his employees. He believed in paying his employees well and offering them good benefit packages. Sinegal believed if you pay people well, "You get good people and good productivity."[3] You also get employee loyalty. Costco has by far the lowest employee turnover rate in all of retailing.

But Sinegal's leadership style of adding value didn't end with employee compensation. He went out of his way to show Costco workers that he cared about them. He maintained an open-door policy with everyone. He wore an employee name tag, was on a first-name basis with everyone, and made sure to visit every single Costco store at least once a year.

"No manager and no staff in any business feels very good if the boss is not interested enough to come and see them," said Sinegal. "The employees know that I want to say hello to them, because I like them."[4]

The only real criticism of Sinegal came from Wall Street. Analysts there believed that Sinegal was too kind and generous to his people. They wanted him to pay employees less and squeeze them more. But Sinegal wouldn't think of it. He believed that if you treat the employees and customers right, profits will follow. "On Wall Street," he observed, "they're in the business of making money between now and next Thursday. I don't say that with any bitterness, but we can't take that view. We want to build a company that will still be here 50 and 60 years from now."[5]

When it came down to it, Sinegal was more focused on adding value to people by serving them than on serving himself. "It's improper for one person to take credit when it takes so many people to build a successful organization," stated Sinegal.[6] He lived by the

Law of Addition. He said, "I just think that if you're going to try to run an organization that's very cost-conscious, then you can't have those disparities. Having an individual who is making 100 or 200 or 300 times more than the average person working on the floor is wrong."[7] Sinegal summed it up this way: "This is not altruistic. This is good business." He could also say it's good leadership!

OBSERVE

The interaction between every leader and follower is a relationship, and all relationships either add to or subtract from a person's life. If you are a leader, then trust me, you are having either a positive or a negative impact on the people you lead.

1 How did Sinegal add value to the employees of Costco?

_____

_____

_____

_____

_____

2 What is Sinegal's return on his investment in his employees?

_____

_____

_____

_____

_____

3 Why should leaders lead? When they do, what is their first responsibility?

_____

_____

_____

_____

_____

4 Does a leader's motive matter, or is it simply getting the job done that's important? What's the bottom line?

_____

_____

_____

_____

5 How do you respond differently to a leader who serves self versus a leader who serves the team?

_____

_____

_____

_____

LEARN

As I try to live out the Law of Addition, I follow four guidelines that help me add value to others. I believe we can add value to others when we . . .

1. TRULY VALUE OTHERS

Becoming a leader means to give up our right to think of ourselves first. We need to focus on others. We must value people and demonstrate our caring in a way that our followers know it. I'm told that in American Sign Language, the sign for serving is to hold the hands out in front with the palms up and to move them back and forth between the signer and the signee. And really, that is a good metaphor for the attitude that servant leaders should possess: they should be open, trusting, caring, offering their help, and willing to be vulnerable. Leaders who add value by serving believe in their people before their people believe in them and serve others before they are served.

2. MAKE OURSELVES MORE VALUABLE TO OTHERS

The whole idea of adding value to other people depends on the idea that you have something of value to add. You can't give what you do not possess. What do you have to give others? Can you teach skills? Can you give opportunities? Can you offer insight and perspective gained through experience? None of these things comes without a price.

If you have skills, you gained them through study and practice. If you have opportunities to give, you acquired them through hard work. If you possess wisdom, you gained it by intentionally evaluating the experiences you've had. The more intentional you have been in growing personally, the more you have to offer. The more you continue to pursue personal growth, the more you will continue to have to offer.

3. Know and Relate to What Others Value

Inexperienced leaders are quick to lead before knowing anything about the people they intend to lead. But mature leaders listen, learn, and then lead. They *listen* to learn their people's stories. They find out about their hopes and dreams. They become acquainted with their aspirations. And they pay attention to their emotions. From those things, they *learn* who their people are and what is valuable to them. And *then* they *lead* based upon what they've learned. When they do that, everybody wins—the organization, the leader, and the followers.

4. Do Things That God Values

This final value may not be for you. If so, just skip it. But for me it's nonnegotiable. I believe that God desires us not only to treat people with respect but also to actively reach out to them and serve them. Scripture provides many examples and descriptions of how we should conduct ourselves, but here is my favorite, captured by Eugene Peterson's *The Message*:

> "When he finally arrives, blazing in beauty and all his angels with him, the Son of Man will take his place on his glorious throne. Then all the nations will be arranged before him and he will sort the people out, much as a shepherd sorts out sheep and goats, putting sheep to his right and goats to his left.
>
> "Then the King will say to those on his right, 'Enter, you who are blessed by my Father! Take what's coming to you in this kingdom. It's been ready for you since the world's foundation. And here's why:
>
> I was hungry and you fed me,
> I was thirsty and you gave me a drink,

I was homeless and you gave me a room,

I was shivering and you gave me clothes,

I was sick and you stopped to visit,

I was in prison and you came to me."

"Then those 'sheep' are going to say, 'Master, what are you talking about? When did we ever see you hungry and feed you, thirsty and give you a drink? And when did we ever see you sick or in prison and come to you?' Then the King will say, 'I'm telling the solemn truth: Whenever you did one of these things to someone overlooked or ignored, that was me—you did it to me.'"

That standard for my conduct influences everything I do, not just in my leadership, but *especially* my leadership. Because the more power I have, the greater my impact on others—for better or worse. And I always want to be someone who adds value to others, not takes it away. God values people so much that when we add value to them, he takes it personally!

DISCUSS

Answer the following questions and discuss your answers when you meet with your team.

1 What does it mean to "add value" to someone?

_____

_____

_____

_____

2 How has someone has added value to you?

_____

_____

_____

_____

_____

3 What evidence can you point to that supports the positive influence you've had on someone you led?

_____

_____

_____

_____

4 What steps have you taken—or will you take—to understand what the people on your team value?

_____

_____

_____

_____

5 How can your own personal growth help you to better serve the people on your team?

_____

_____

_____

_____

APPLY

1 Do you have a servant's attitude when it comes to leadership? Don't be too quick to say yes. Here's how you can tell. In situations where you are required to serve others' needs, how do you respond? Do you become impatient? Do you feel resentful? Do you believe that certain tasks are beneath you or your position? If you answer yes to any of those questions, then your attitude is not as good as it could be. Make it a practice to perform small acts of service for others without seeking credit or recognition for them. Continue until you no longer resent doing them.

_____

_____

_____

_____

2 Do you value what the people closest to you value? Make a list of the most important people in your life, both personal and professional. Beside each name, write what that person values most. Then rate yourself on a scale of 1 (poorly) to 10 (excellently) for how actively and intentionally you support the person in that area.

_____

_____

_____

3 Make adding value part of your lifestyle. Begin with those closest to you. How could you add value to the people on your list related to what *they* value? Start doing it. Then do the same with all the people you lead. If there are only a few, add value individually. If you lead large numbers of people, you may have to think of ways to serve groups as well as individuals.

_____

_____

_____

TAKE ACTION

What do you have to give others? Can you teach skills? Can you give opportunities? Can you give insight and perspective gained through experience? You can add value to *someone*. List below the name of the person you will add value to over the next few months and fill in the related phrase. Then set up a consistent time to meet with this person.

I will mentor:

_____

Why I chose this person:

_____

What I have to offer this person:

_____

Three ways I can add to this person's life:

_____

_____

_____

We will meet (once each / every other) week for ___ months.

6

❖❖

THE LAW OF SOLID GROUND

Trust Is the Foundation of Leadership

How important is trust for a leader? It is *the most important* thing. Trust is the foundation of leadership. It is the glue that holds people together on a team, in an organization, and even in a nation. Leaders cannot repeatedly break trust with people and continue to influence them. Violate the Law of Solid Ground, and you diminish your influence as a leader. But honor the law and build trust, and people will follow you even through the toughest of situations.

READ

In my lifetime, I've observed the gradual breakdown of trust in our society, especially of its leaders. In the fifties and early sixties, people had confidence in political leaders and the federal government. At that time, nearly 80 percent of Americans believed the federal government could be trusted to do the right thing most of the time.[1] Today, only 24 percent of Americans trust the government.[2] In a 2020 Gallup poll, people identified members of Congress as the *least* honest and ethical group by profession, with only 8 percent of people believing members of Congress demonstrated high or very high trustworthiness.[3] When did trust in government leaders begin to erode? I believe it started in the mid- and late-sixties during the Vietnam War.

In 1961 during President John F. Kennedy's first year in office, when he said he wanted to fight and contain communism by supporting South Vietnam, most Americans supported him. Though he originally planned to provide only aid, that year he also sent four hundred Green Beret commandos to Vietnam as advisors.[4] The next year he sent an additional twelve thousand military "advisors" as well as three hundred helicopters and pilots.[5] President Lyndon B. Johnson, who took office following Kennedy's assassination, escalated American involvement in the war. In 1965, he sent one hundred fifty thousand troops.[6] By 1966, more than two hundred thousand Americans had been sent to Vietnam. Even with reports of casualties rising, two-thirds of all Americans surveyed by Louis Harris believed that Vietnam was the place where the United States should "stand and fight communism." And most people expressed the belief that the US should stay until the fight was finished.

If you know anything about the sixties, you know that the War in Vietnam divided the country. It sparked protests, inspired a huge antiwar movement, and brought about radical social change. How did the country move from overwhelming support to overwhelming opposition? The people lost trust in the nation's leaders.

Johnson and his secretary of defense, Robert McNamara, weren't honest with the American people about the war. As early as 1962, McNamara told the public they were winning the war.[7] In his book *In Retrospect*, McNamara recounted that he repeatedly minimized American losses and told only half-truths about the war. For example, he said, "Upon my return to Washington [from Saigon] on December 21, [1963,] I was less than candid when I reported to the press . . . I said, 'We observed the results of a very substantial increase in Vietcong activity' (true); but I then added, 'We reviewed the plans of the South Vietnamese and we have every reason to believe they will be successful' (an overstatement at best)."[8]

For a while, nobody questioned McNamara's statements because there was no reason to mistrust the country's leaders. But in time, people recognized that his words and the facts weren't matching up. More and more young men were being drafted and sent to Vietnam, yet they were losing the war. The American public began to lose faith. Years later, McNamara admitted his failure: "We of the Kennedy and Johnson administrations who participated in the decisions on Vietnam acted according to what we thought were the principles and traditions of this nation. We made our decisions in light of those values. Yet we were wrong, terribly wrong."[9] The era that had begun with the hope and idealism characterized by John F. Kennedy ultimately ended with the mistrust and cynicism associated with Richard Nixon following Watergate and Nixon's resignation.

Whenever a leader breaks the Law of Solid Ground, he pays a price in his leadership. And the people who are asked to follow him suffer too. The repercussions of broken trust that started to rise in the sixties continue today, not only with political leaders, but with leaders in business, religious institutions, and the entertainment industry. Why? Because they have broken trust.

OBSERVE

Craig Weatherup, who retired as founding chairman and CEO of the Pepsi Bottling Group, said, "People will tolerate honest mistakes, but if you violate their trust you will find it very difficult to ever regain their confidence. That is one reason that you need to treat trust as your most precious asset. You may fool your boss but you can never fool your colleagues or subordinates."

1 How did Robert McNamara violate the trust of the American people?

_____

_____

_____

_____

2 How did McNamara and Johnson's actions reflect on the rest of the American government?

_____

_____

_____

_____

3 Think of a time when a leader violated your trust. What was your reaction?

_____

_____

_____

_____

4 After your trust has been violated, how is it regained?

_____

_____

_____

_____

_____

_____

5 Can you think of instances in which you have violated your followers' trust? If so, how will you work to restore that trust?

_____

_____

_____

_____

_____

_____

LEARN

I've become well known for teaching that everything rises and falls on leadership. Everything rises when leaders demonstrate competence and good values. Everything falls when leaders demonstrate incompetence and poor values. Why do I say this? When leaders lack competence, they can't accomplish anything. When leaders lack good values, they can't be trusted. They lack character. Without both competence and good values, they can't get anyone to follow them.

Character and competence always go hand in hand. Journalist and former president of the U.S. Business and Industrial Council Anthony Harrigan said,

The role of character always has been the key factor in the rise and fall of nations. And one can be sure that America is no exception to this rule of history. We won't survive as a country because we are smarter or more sophisticated but because we are—we hope—stronger inwardly. In short, character is the only effective bulwark against internal and external forces that lead to a country's disintegration or collapse.

Character and good values make trust possible. And trust makes leadership possible. Whenever you lead people, it's as if they consent to take a journey with you. The way that trip is going to turn out is predicted by your character. Because no one enjoys spending time with someone they don't trust.

CHARACTER COMMUNICATES CONSISTENCY

Leaders without inner strength can't be counted on day after day because their ability to perform changes constantly. NBA great Jerry West commented, "You can't get too much done in life if you only work on the days when you feel good." If your people don't know what to expect from you as a leader, at some point they won't look to you for leadership.

When I think of leaders who epitomize consistency of character, the first person who comes to mind is Billy Graham. Regardless of personal religious beliefs, people trusted him. Why? Because he modeled high character for more than half a century. He lived out his values every day. He never made a commitment unless he was going to keep it. And he went out of his way to personify integrity.

CHARACTER COMMUNICATES POTENTIAL

British politician and writer John Morley observed, "No man can climb out beyond the limitations of his own character." Weak character is limiting. Who do you think has the greater potential to achieve great dreams and have a positive impact on others: someone who is honest, disciplined, and hardworking, or someone who is deceitful, impulsive, and lazy? It sounds obvious when it's phrased that way, doesn't it?

Poor character is like a time bomb ticking away. It's only a matter of time before it blows up a person's ability to perform and the capacity to lead. Why? Because people with weak character are not trustworthy, and trust is the foundation of leadership. Craig Weatherup explained, "You don't build trust by talking about it. You build it by achieving results, always with integrity and in a manner that shows real personal regard for the people with whom you work."[10]

When leaders have strong character, people trust them, and they trust in their ability to release their potential. That not only gives their followers hope for the future, but it also promotes a strong belief in themselves and their organization.

CHARACTER COMMUNICATES RESPECT

When you don't have character within, you can't earn respect without. And respect is absolutely essential for lasting leadership. How do leaders earn respect? By making tough decisions, by admitting their mistakes, and by putting what's best for their followers and the organization ahead of their personal agendas. Respect is earned on difficult ground.

Years ago a movie was made about the Fifty-Fourth Massachusetts Infantry regiment and its colonel, Robert Gould Shaw. The film was called *Glory*, and though some of its plot was fictionalized, the Civil War story of Shaw's journey with his men—and of the respect he earned from them—was real.

The movie recounted the formation of this unit in the Union army, which was the first to be composed of Black soldiers. Shaw, a white officer, took command of the regiment, oversaw recruiting, selected the (white) officers, equipped the men, and trained them as soldiers. He drove them hard, knowing that their performance in battle would either vindicate or condemn the value of Black people as soldiers and citizens in the minds of many white Northerners. In the process, the soldiers and Shaw earned one another's respect.

A few months after their training was complete, the men of the Fifty-Fourth got the opportunity to prove themselves in the Union assault on Confederate Fort Wagner in South Carolina. Shaw's biographer Russell Duncan said of the attack: "With a final admonition to 'prove yourselves men,' Shaw positioned himself in front and ordered, 'Forward.' Years later, one soldier remembered that the regiment fought hard because Shaw was in front, not behind."[11]

Almost half of the six hundred men from the Fifty-Fourth who fought that day were wounded, captured, or killed. Though they fought valiantly, they were unable to take Fort Wagner. And Shaw, who had courageously led his men to the top of the fort's parapet in the first assault, was killed among his men.

Shaw's actions on that final day solidified the respect his men already had for him. Two weeks after the battle, Albanus Fisher, a sergeant in the Fifty-Fourth, said, "I still feel more Eager for the struggle than I ever yet have, for I now wish to have Revenge for our galant Curnel [*sic*]."[12] J. R. Miller once observed, "The only thing that walks back from the tomb with the mourners and refuses to be buried is the character of a man. This is true. What a man is survives him. It can never be buried." Shaw's character, strong to the last, had communicated a level of respect to his men that lived beyond him.

DISCUSS

Answer the following questions and discuss your answers when you meet with your team.

1   Do you agree with the statement that to build trust, a leader must exemplify competence, connection, and character? Can you gain trust without one of these characteristics? Is there another characteristic you would add? Explain.

_____

_____

_____

_____

_____

2   How effective will a leader be if he or she has lost the trust of the team?

_____

_____

_____

_____

3   How does character communicate consistency, potential, and respect? Give an example for each.

_____

_____

_____

_____

_____

4   What is the quickest way for a person to lose your trust?

_____

_____

_____

_____

5 How would you handle a situation in which you worked with someone you didn't trust?

_____

_____

_____

_____

6 How do you gain and maintain the trust of others?

_____

_____

_____

7 Of the three trust-building factors–competence, connection, character–which is your strength? In which are you the weakest? Why?

_____

_____

_____

_____

APPLY

1 How can you measure your people's trust in you? By gauging how open they are with you. Do your team members openly share opinions with you—even negative ones? Do they give you bad news as readily as good news? Do they *volunteer* information about their areas of responsibility? If not, they may not trust your character. How about your leaders? Do they consistently put their trust in you? Do they regularly give you weight to carry? If so, they trust you. If not, you need to work on your competence, your character, or both.

_____

_____

_____

_____

2 How can you improve your character? I recommend that you focus on three main values: integrity, authenticity, and discipline. To develop your integrity, make a commitment to yourself to be scrupulously honest. Don't shave the truth, don't tell white lies, and don't fudge numbers. Be truthful even when it hurts. To develop authenticity, be yourself with everyone. Don't play politics, role-play, or pretend to be anything you're not. To strengthen your discipline, do the right things every day regardless of how you feel.

_____

_____

_____

_____

_____

3 If you have broken trust with others in the past, then you must try to make things right. First, apologize to whomever you have hurt or betrayed. If you can make amends or restitution, then do so. And commit to work at re-earning people's trust. The greater the violation, the longer it will take. The onus is not on them to trust. The onus is on you to earn trust back.

_____

_____

_____

_____

_____

TAKE ACTION

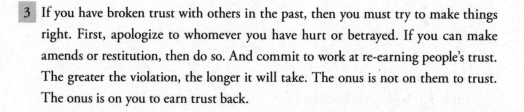

When you work with others, you have a number of opportunities to display your competence, connection, and character in the decisions you make and actions you take. With every decision and action, you are either gaining or losing change, building or losing trust. Take time to evaluate your current level of trust with the team you are leading or working with now.

1 Overall, how would your team rate your competence—high or low? Explain.

_____

_____

_____

_____

_____

_____

2 Have there been times when mistakes you made held the team back? If so, how do you think it has damaged people's trust in you? How can you repair it?

_____

_____

_____

_____

_____

_____

3 List the names of the people on your team. Next to each name, give a brief example of how you have made an effort to connect with that person.

_____

_____

_____

_____

_____

_____

4 How does your level of connection affect your ability to lead or work with the people you listed? Who should you spend more time connecting with? How do you plan to do this?

_____

_____

_____

_____

5 Give yourself a grade on a scale of 1–10 (one being an area of weakness and 10 being an area of strength) on each of the following character areas:

Commitment	1	2	3	4	5	6	7	8	9	10
Courage	1	2	3	4	5	6	7	8	9	10
Honesty	1	2	3	4	5	6	7	8	9	10
Perseverance	1	2	3	4	5	6	7	8	9	10
Preparedness	1	2	3	4	5	6	7	8	9	10
Respect for others	1	2	3	4	5	6	7	8	9	10
Responsibility	1	2	3	4	5	6	7	8	9	10
Self-discipline	1	2	3	4	5	6	7	8	9	10
Teachability	1	2	3	4	5	6	7	8	9	10
Unselfishness	1	2	3	4	5	6	7	8	9	10

To better evaluate your character, talk to someone in your work environment whom you trust and who can honestly give you feedback about what areas of your character or how you express yourself you can work on.

7

✦✦✦

THE LAW OF RESPECT

People Naturally Follow Better Leaders Than Themselves

When people respect you as a person, they *admire* you. When they respect you as a friend, they *love* you. When they respect you as a leader, they *follow* you. There are different forms and levels of respect, and if you want to influence others, you need to be respected as a leader. And in order to do that, you will have to prove yourself and your abilities as stated by the Law of Respect. As Clarence B. Randall said, "The leader must know, must know he knows, and must be able to make it abundantly clear to those around him that he knows."

READ

If you had seen her, your first reaction might not have been respect. She wasn't a very impressive-looking person—just a little over five feet tall, in her late thirties, with dark brown weathered skin. She couldn't read or write. The clothes she wore were coarse and worn. When she smiled, it revealed that her top two front teeth were missing.

She lived alone. The story was that she had abandoned her husband when she was twenty-nine. She gave him no warning. One day he woke up, and she was gone.

Her employment was erratic. Most of the time she took domestic jobs in small hotels: scrubbing floors, making up rooms, and cooking. Just about every spring and fall she would disappear from her place of employment, come back broke, and work again to scrape together funds. When she was present on the job, she worked hard and seemed physically tough, but she also was known to suddenly fall asleep—sometimes in the middle of a conversation. She attributed her affliction to a blow to the head she had taken during a teenage fight.

Who would respect someone like that? The more than three hundred slaves who followed her to freedom out of the South—they recognized and respected her leadership. So did just about every abolitionist in New England. The year was 1857. The woman's name was Harriet Tubman.

While she was only in her thirties, Harriet Tubman came to be called Moses because of her ability to go into the land of captivity and bring back so many people out of slavery's bondage. Tubman started life as a slave. Born in 1820, she grew up in the farmland of Maryland. When she was thirteen, she received the blow to her head that troubled her all her life. A white overseer in a store demanded her assistance so that he could beat an escaping slave. When she refused and blocked his way, the white man threw a two-pound weight that hit Tubman in the head. She nearly died, and her recovery took months.

At age twenty-four, she married John Tubman, a free Black man. But when she talked to him about escaping to freedom in the North, he wouldn't hear of it. He said if she tried to leave, he'd turn her in. When she resolved to take her chances and go north in 1849, she did so alone, without a word to him. Her first biographer, Sarah Bradford, said that Tubman told her: "I had reasoned this out in my mind: there was one of two things I had a *right* to, liberty or death. If I could not have one, I would have the other, for no man should take me alive. I should fight for my liberty as my strength lasted."

Tubman made her way to Philadelphia, Pennsylvania, via the Underground Railroad, a secret network of free Blacks, white abolitionists, and Quakers who helped escaping slaves on the run. Though free herself, she vowed to return to Maryland and bring her family out. In 1850, she made her first return trip as an Underground Railroad "conductor"—someone who retrieved and guided out slaves with the assistance of sympathizers along the way.

Each summer and winter, Tubman worked to make return trips to the South. Every spring and fall, she risked her life by going south and returning with more people. She was fearless, and her leadership was unshakable. Hers was extremely dangerous work, and when people in her charge wavered or had second thoughts, she was strong as steel. Tubman knew escaped slaves who returned would be beaten and tortured until they gave information about those who had helped them. So she never allowed any of the people she was guiding to give up. "Dead folks tell no tales," she would tell a fainthearted slave as she put a loaded pistol to his head. "You go on or die!"

Between 1850 and 1860, Harriet Tubman guided out more than three hundred people, including many of her family members. She made nineteen trips in all and was proud of the fact that she never once lost a single person under her care. "I never ran my train off the track," she said, "and I never lost a passenger." At the time, southern whites put a $12,000 price on her head—that would be around $400,000 today.[1] By the start of the Civil War, she had brought more people out of slavery than any other American in history—Black or white, male or female.

Tubman's reputation and influence commanded respect, and not just among slaves who dreamed of gaining freedom. Influential Northerners of both races sought her out. She spoke at rallies and in homes throughout Philadelphia, Pennsylvania; Boston, Massachusetts; St. Catharines, Canada; and Auburn, New York, where she eventually settled. People of prominence sought her out, such as Senator William Seward, who later became Abraham Lincoln's secretary of state, and outspoken abolitionist and former slave Frederick Douglass. Tubman's advice and leadership were also requested by John Brown, the famed revolutionary abolitionist. Brown always referred to the former slave as "General Tubman," and he was quoted as saying she "was a better officer than most whom he had seen, and could command an army as successfully as she had led her small parties of fugitives."[2] That is the essence of the Law of Respect.

OBSERVE

Harriet Tubman would appear to be an unlikely candidate for leadership because the deck was certainly stacked against her. She was uneducated. She began life as a slave. She lived in a culture that didn't respect Black people. And she labored in a country where women didn't have the right to vote yet. Despite her circumstances, she became an incredible leader. The reason is simple: people naturally follow better leaders than themselves. Everyone who came in contact with her recognized her strong leadership ability and felt compelled to follow her. That's how the Law of Respect works.

1 Why wasn't Harriet Tubman an obvious choice as a leader?

_____

_____

_____

2 How did Harriet Tubman gain respect?

_____

_____

_____

_____

3 How did respect factor into her leadership abilities?

_____

_____

_____

_____

4 Who is the person you respect the most in your profession? Why is this person so highly respected? What has this person been able to accomplish

_____

_____

_____

_____

5 Who do you most respect in your organization? Why?

_____

_____

_____

_____

LEARN

People don't follow others by accident. They follow individuals whose leadership they respect. People who are an 8 in leadership (on a scale from 1 to 10, with 10 being the strongest) don't go out and look for a 6 to follow—they naturally follow a 9 or 10. The less skilled follow the more highly skilled and gifted. Occasionally, a strong leader may choose to follow someone less effective than himself. But when that happens, it's for a reason. For example, the better leader may do it out of respect for the person's office or past accomplishments.

Or he may be following the chain of command. In general, though, followers are attracted to people who are better leaders than themselves. That is the Law of Respect.

When people get together for the first time in a group, take a look at what happens. As they start interacting, the better leaders emerge, and they begin to influence the others. At first, many people may make tentative moves in several different directions, but after the people get to know one another, it doesn't take long for them to recognize the best leaders and to start following them.

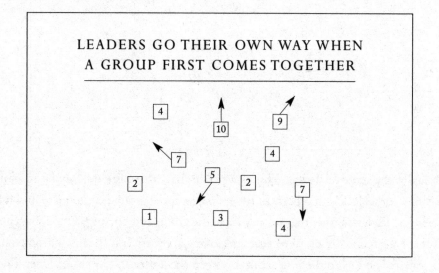

LEADERS GO THEIR OWN WAY WHEN A GROUP FIRST COMES TOGETHER

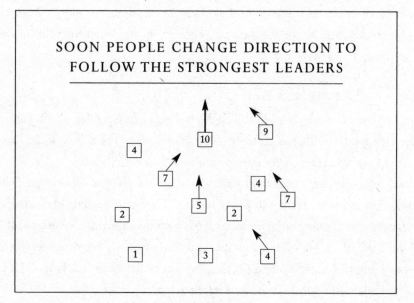

SOON PEOPLE CHANGE DIRECTION TO FOLLOW THE STRONGEST LEADERS

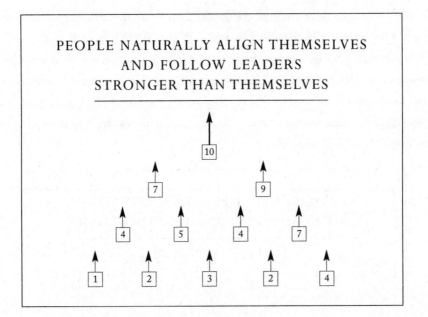

Usually the more leadership ability a person has, the more quickly he recognizes leadership—or its lack—in others. In time, people in the group get on board and follow the strongest leaders. Either that or they leave the group and pursue their own agenda.

What causes one person to respect and follow another? Is it because of the qualities of the leader? Is it due to the interaction between the leader and follower? Does it occur because of circumstances? I believe all those factors can come into play and more. Based on my observations and personal experience, here are the top seven ways that leaders gain others' respect:

1. NATURAL LEADERSHIP ABILITY

First and foremost is leadership ability. All leaders are not created equal. Some people are born with greater skills and ability to lead. However, as I've stated in the Law of the Lid and the Law of Process, every person can become a better leader.

If you possess natural leadership ability, people will want to follow you. They will want to be around you. They will listen to you. They will become excited when you communicate vision. However, natural leadership ability alone is not enough. If you do not exhibit some of the additional practices and characteristics listed below, you will not reach your leadership capacity, and people may not continue to follow you. One of the greatest potential pitfalls for natural leaders is relying on talent alone.

2. RESPECT FOR OTHERS

The one common characteristic all leaders possess is the ability to see more than others and before others. This gives leaders an advantage. Dictators and other autocratic leaders use this ability to gain power and benefit themselves, and they often rely on violence and intimidation to keep it. Leaders with poor values use their advantage to exploit and manipulate others.

In contrast, respect for others sets good leaders apart from bad ones. Good leaders understand that much of leadership is voluntary. When leaders show respect for others—especially for people who have less power or a lower position than theirs—they gain respect. As a result, people *want* to follow them, because the more respect they have for someone, the more open they are to their leadership.

Gaining respect from others follows a pattern:

When people respect you as a person, they *admire* you.
When they respect you as a friend, they *love* you.
When they respect you as a leader, they *follow* you.

If you continually respect others and consistently lead them well, you will continue to have followers.

3. DIFFICULTIES OVERCOME

Respect is gained on difficult ground. Any time leaders care enough about people to positively confront them to help them solve a problem, overcome a blind spot, or change a destructive behavior, both of them grow. The leaders grow in the respect they've earned. The followers grow because they experience breakthroughs they might otherwise never experience.

I've seen this over and over with the corporate clients I've mentored. When I teach leaders how to have candid conversations tackling difficult subjects with team members, the clients have come back and told us those were the most valuable skills they've learned. The conversations they had revolutionized their leadership, and they want more mentoring on how to tackle tough conversations.

4. COURAGE

People do not follow titles; they follow courage. One of the reasons everyone respected Harriet Tubman so much was her tremendous courage. She was determined to succeed, or she was going to die trying. She didn't let the danger stop her. Her mission was clear, and she was absolutely fearless.

Former US secretary of state Henry Kissinger remarked, "A leader does not deserve the name unless he is willing occasionally to stand alone." Good leaders do what's right, even at the risk of failure, in the face of great danger, and under the brunt of relentless criticism. I can't think of even one great leader from history who was without courage. Can you? A leader's courage has great value: it gives followers hope.

5. Success

Success is very attractive. People are naturally drawn to it. It's one reason why people in our society are so focused on celebrities' lives, cheer for their favorite sports team, and follow the careers of music stars.

Success is even more important when it applies to the people who lead us. People respect others' accomplishments. And it's hard to argue with a good track record. When leaders are successful in their own endeavors, people respect them. When they succeed in leading the team to victory, then followers believe they can do it again. As a result, followers follow them because they want to be part of success in the future.

6. Loyalty

We live in an era of free agency. The average worker, according to one source, will change occupations ten times by the time he reaches age thirty-six.[3] Professional athletes hop from team to team, looking for the best deal. CEOs negotiate ridiculously high financial packages, but when things go wrong, they bail out as millionaires.

In a culture of constant change, turnover, and transition, loyalty is an asset. When leaders stick with the team until the job is done, remain loyal to the organization when the going gets rough, and look out for followers even when it hurts them, followers respect them and their actions.

7. Value Added to Others

Perhaps the greatest source of respect for a leader comes from his or her dedication to adding value to others. Because I've already discussed this extensively in the Law of Addition, I probably don't need to say much here. But you can be sure that followers value leaders who add value to them. And their respect for them carries on long after the relationship has ended.

If you want to measure how much respect you have as a leader, the first thing you should do is to look at who you attract. Dennis A. Peer remarked, "One measure of leadership is the caliber of people who choose to follow you." The second thing you should do is to see how your people respond when you ask for commitment or change.

When leaders are respected and they ask for commitment, their people sign up and step up. They are ready to take risks, put in long hours, or do whatever else is necessary to get the job done. Likewise, when respected leaders ask for change, followers are willing to embrace it. But when leaders who are not respected ask for commitment or change, people doubt, they question, they make excuses, or they simply walk away. It is very hard for a leader who hasn't earned respect to get other people to follow when it's not easy or convenient.

DISCUSS

Answer the following questions and discuss your answers when you meet with your team.

1 Under what circumstances would a strong leader follow a weaker leader?

_____

_____

_____

2 What are the three phases that most groups go through when they first come together?

_____

_____

_____

3 Do you agree that in most cases people choose to follow leaders who they respect? Explain.

_____

_____

_____

_____

4 How do you determine the strongest leader in the group?

_____

_____

_____

_____

5 From your own experience or observation, what happens when two strong leaders are placed in the same group?

_____

_____

_____

_____

6 Think about a current group in which you are voluntarily participating. Why is the person who is leading the group the leader? What form of respect do you have for the leader (position, friend, admiration, leadership, past accomplishments)?

_____

_____

_____

_____

7 How do you react when you are placed in a group of strong leaders?

_____

_____

_____

_____

8 What are you doing (or what will you start to do) to increase your level or respect among the people you interact with often or daily?

_____

_____

_____

_____

APPLY

1   Think about the last time you asked employees, followers, or volunteers for commitment or asked them to change something they were doing. What was their response? If they gladly followed, they probably respect your leadership. If they resisted, they may not.

_____

_____

_____

_____

_____

2   Take a look at the qualities that help a leader to gain respect:

- Leadership ability (natural ability)
- Respect for others
- Courage
- Success record
- Faithfulness
- Value added to others

Rank yourself in each area on a scale of 1 (low) to 10 (high). One of the best ways to raise your "leadership number" is to improve in each area. For each entry, write a practice, habit, or goal that will help you to improve in that area. Then work for a month on each to create improvement in that area. (Note: you will need to work much longer to gain a good success record.)

3   One of my favorite definitions of success is having the respect of those closest to me. I believe that if my family (who knows me the best) and my closest coworkers (who work with me every day) have respect for me, then I am successful.

_____

_____

_____

_____

If you have the courage, ask the people closest to you what they respect most about you. And ask them to identify areas where you most need to grow. Then strive to improve based on their honest feedback.

TAKE ACTION

Having the respect of those closest to you is priceless. I think success is having the people who know me the best, respect me the most. Respect is not always the result of having other people agree with you, and because we are all unique individuals, we are not going to agree on everything. But gaining the respect of the people who know us the best—our success and failures, beliefs and convictions, strengths and weaknesses, character and motives—is an accomplishment.

This week, gather together three of your friends for a discussion. Come up with at least five situations in which you and your friends might find yourself as a group. (For example, planning a trip, entering a business venture, experiencing a medical emergency, or teaming up to play a sport.) For each situation, have each person tell which person in the group he or she would most likely follow and why. List the situations you and your friends come up with below, and then list the names of who was mentioned as the leader for each situation.

Situation: **Leader:**

_____   _____

_____   _____

_____   _____

_____   _____

_____   _____

_____   _____

_____   _____

From this exercise, recognize that different people take the leadership position at different times depending on their skills, personality, and leadership qualities.

1 Who was named the leader the most times? Why?

_____

_____

_____

_____

2 Who was named the leader the fewest times? Why?

_____

_____

_____

_____

3 How often were you named as the person they would follow? What does that say about your leadership? How could you gain more of their respect?

_____

_____

_____

_____

8

---·•••·---

The Law of Intuition

Leaders Evaluate Everything with a Leadership Bias

O ver the years that I've spoken to audiences about the 21 Laws of Leadership, I've found the Law of Intuition to be the most difficult to teach. When I talk about it, natural leaders get it instantly, learned leaders get it eventually, and non-leaders just look at me blankly. Leaders look at things differently than others do. They evaluate everything according to their leadership bias. Good leaders have a filter that causes them to look for leadership dynamics first to explain results in an organization or on a team. That develops in them a leadership intuition that informs everything they do. It becomes an inseparable part of who they are. And when their intuition is right and they follow it, their leadership goes to entirely new levels.

READ

One of the most remarkable stories of intuition in the last fifty years is that of Apple, Inc. Just about everybody knows about Apple. The company was created in 1976 by Steve Jobs and Steve Wozniak in a garage. Just four years later, the business went public, opening at twenty-two dollars a share and selling 4.6 million shares. It made more than forty employees and investors millionaires overnight.

In the years since then, Apple's success, stock value, and ability to capture customers have fluctuated wildly. Founder Steve Jobs was pushed out of Apple in 1985, but the company was unable to reestablish the success of its glory days when it sold 14.6 percent of all personal computers in the United States. By 1997, sales were down to 3.5 percent. That was when Apple again looked to the leadership of its original founder, Steve Jobs, for help and brought him back.

Jobs intuitively reviewed the situation and immediately took action. He knew that improvement was impossible without a change in leadership, so he quickly dismissed all but two of the previous board members and installed new ones. He made changes in the executive leadership. And he fired the company's ad agency and held a competition for the account among three firms.

He also refocused the company. Jobs wanted to get back to the basics of what Apple had always done best: use its individuality to create products that made a difference. At the time Jobs said, "We've reviewed the road map of new products and axed more than 70% of the projects, keeping the 30% that were gems. Plus we're adding new ones that are a whole new paradigm of looking at computers."[1]

At that time, many computer manufacturers were working to create personal digital assistants (PDAs). Jobs followed his intuition and was busy inventing a new way for people to listen to music. In 2001, he launched the iPod and the Apple music store. Ben Knauss, who was on the inside of that project, said, "The interesting thing about the iPod, is that since it started, it had 100 percent of Steve Jobs' time. Not many projects get that. He was heavily involved in every single aspect of the project."[2] Why did Jobs do that? Because his intuition as a leader made him understand the impact that the device could make. It was consistent with his vision for creating a digital lifestyle. Within four years, Apple possessed 75 percent of the world market for digital music players![3]

In 2007, Jobs launched the iPhone, which created an even bigger digital revolution. Not only did the iPhone make PDAs and MP3 players like the iPod obsolete, it changed the way people lived and interacted. Sadly, Jobs died of cancer in 2011, but the company was already on an incredible trajectory. In 2013, Apple, Inc. was named the most valuable company in the world. It remained at the top for five consecutive years.[4] And it continues to innovate without Jobs. In 2015, it introduced the Apple Watch. Nearly half of all the smartwatches ever sold in the world have been manufactured by Apple.[5]

OBSERVE

The story of Steve Jobs and Apple is a reminder that leadership is really more art than science. The principles of leadership are constant, but the application changes with every leader and every situation. That's why it requires intuition. Without it, leaders get blindsided, and that's one of the worst things that can happen to a leader. If you want to lead long, lead well, and stay ahead of others, you've got to obey the Law of Intuition.

1 What actions did Steve Jobs take that demonstrated his intuition in leadership?

_____

_____

_____

_____

2 How would you define intuition?

_____

_____

_____

3 How does the amount of time a leader has to make a decision relate to the Law of Intuition?

_____

_____

_____

4 In your profession or area of service, how has leadership intuition accelerated the success of one organization over another?

_____

_____

_____

_____

LEARN

Because of their intuition, leaders evaluate everything with a leadership bias. People born with natural leadership ability are especially strong in the area of leadership intuition. Others have to work hard to develop and hone it. But either way, intuition comes from two things: learned skills and natural ability, which comes in a person's areas of strength. It is an informed intuition, and it causes leadership issues to jump out to a leader in a way that they don't with others.

I regard leadership intuition as the ability of a leader to read what's going on. For that reason, I say that leaders are readers:

LEADERS ARE READERS OF THEIR SITUATION

In all kinds of circumstances, leaders pick up on details that might elude others. They "tune in" to leadership dynamics. Many leaders describe this as an ability to "smell" things in their organization. They can sense people's attitudes. They are able to measure the chemistry of a team. They can tell when things are humming and when they're winding down—or getting ready to grind to a halt. They don't need to sift through stats, read reports, or examine the balance sheet. They know the situation *before* they have all the facts. That is the result of their leadership intuition.

As I explained in the Law of Navigation, leaders see more and before others. They intuitively see and understand the big picture, the opportunity, the future. And they sense these things before others around them are aware of them. That's what Jamie Kern Lima did. She understood that women everywhere wanted makeup and skin products that work for them, not just for beautiful models in their twenties. That's why she started IT in her living room and was able to sell it as a billion-dollar business less than a decade later. Her intuition was so dead-on correct, that in the first two years IT was owned by L'Oréal, its revenue nearly *doubled*![6] Kern Lima read the situation and followed her intuition, and time proved her right.

LEADERS ARE READERS OF TRENDS

Most workers are focused on their current work. They think in terms of tasks at hand, projects, or specific goals. That is as it should be. Most managers are concerned with efficiency and effectiveness. They often possess a broader view than employees, thinking in terms of processes over weeks, months, or even years. But leaders take an even broader view. They look at years, decades, and even generations ahead.

Everything that happens around us does so in the context of a bigger picture. Leaders have the ability—and responsibility—to step back from what's happening at the moment and to discern not only where the organization has been, but also where it is headed. Sometimes they can accomplish this through analysis, but often the best leaders sense it first and find data to explain it later. Their intuition tells them that something is happening, that conditions are changing, and that trouble or opportunity is coming. Leaders must always be a few steps ahead of their best people, or they're not really leading. They can do that only if they are able to read trends.

LEADERS ARE READERS OF THEIR RESOURCES

A major difference between leaders and everyone else is the way they see resources. A good worker encounters a challenge and thinks, *What can I do to help?* A high achiever asks, *How can I solve this problem?* A peak performer wonders, *What must I do to reach the next level so that I can overcome this?*

Leaders think differently. They think in terms of resources and how to maximize them. They see a challenge, problem, or opportunity, and they think, *Who is the best person to take this on? What resources—raw materials, technology, information, people, and so forth—can help us? What will this take financially? How can I encourage my team to achieve success?*

Leaders see everything with a leadership bias. Their focus is on mobilizing people and leveraging resources to achieve their goals rather than on just using their own individual efforts. Leaders who want to succeed maximize every asset and resource they have for the benefit of their organization. For that reason, they are continually aware of what they have at their disposal.

LEADERS ARE READERS OF PEOPLE

President Lyndon Johnson once said that when you walk into a room, you don't belong in politics if you can't tell who's for you and who's against you. That statement also applies to any other kind of leader. Intuitive leaders can sense what's happening among people and know their hopes, fears, and concerns.

Reading people is perhaps the most important intuitive skill leaders can possess.

After all, if what you are doing doesn't involve people, it's not leadership. And if you aren't influencing people to follow, you aren't really leading.

LEADERS ARE READERS OF THEMSELVES

Finally, good leaders develop the ability to read themselves. Poet James Russell Lowell observed, "No one can produce great things who is not thoroughly sincere in dealing with himself." Leaders must know not only their own strengths and blind spots, skills and weaknesses, but also their current state of mind. Why? Because leaders can hinder progress just as easily as they can help create it. Everything rises and falls on leadership. In fact, it's easier for a bad leader to damage an organization than it is for a good leader to build one. We've all seen excellent organizations that took generations to build fall apart in a matter of years.

When leaders become self-centered, pessimistic, or rigid in their thinking, they often hurt their organizations because they are likely to fall into the trap of thinking they cannot or should not change. And once that happens, the organization has a hard time becoming better. Its decline is inevitable.

HOW TO DEVELOP LEADERSHIP INTUITION

If you're thinking to yourself, *I'd like to be able to read these dynamics in my organization, but I just don't see things intuitively*, don't despair. The good news is that you can improve your leadership intuition, even if you were not born with great leadership gifting. As I've already mentioned, leadership intuition is *informed* intuition. The less natural leadership talent you have, the more you will need to make up for it by developing skills and gaining experience. They can help you to develop thinking patterns, and thinking patterns can be learned. To help you in this process, I'll tell you about the questions I ask myself when reading my leadership intuition: *What do I feel? What do I know? What do I think? What should I do?*

1. WHAT DO I FEEL?

To lean into my intuition, I always start by examining what I feel. When I say that, I don't mean whether I'm happy or sad or angry. I'm talking about my gut, the way Jamie Kern Lima did. What are my instincts? What belief do I possess that perhaps I can't explain using facts? Often I can sense opportunity, but I can't easily put my finger on what it is. This is where I always start, and you should too. Pay attention to your instincts.

2. What do I know?

While I listen to my instincts, I don't rely on them entirely. I test them using what I know. I try to bring as many pieces of information into play as I can. If I need to connect with someone who possesses knowledge I lack, I'll do that. I'll also rely on my past experience. If you have a great track record, this can really help you. If you don't, you would be wise to rely on this less.

3. What do I think?

Here is where I start putting things together. Where do my thinking and knowledge line up? Where do they contradict one another? If they're at odds, why? Sometimes this thinking phase is fast, either affirming or countering my instincts. But often I'll spend days or weeks reflecting before I come to a conclusion.

I need to pause here and give you some guidance about responding to these first three questions before moving on to the final question. I often teach that people are intuitive in the areas of their natural gifting. Because I possess leadership gifting, I lean very heavily into how I feel. How much credence do I give it? Around 80 percent. I follow my leadership instincts as far as I can because I've learned that I can trust them. I temper them with what I know and what I think. If you lack strong leadership gifting—and there's no shame in lacking it, only in pretending you have it—then rely only 20 percent on how you feel, and put 80 percent of your trust in what you know and think.

4. What should I do?

The final question is about action. The first three questions have little value without an answer to this fourth question. Once I've examined my feelings, knowledge, and thinking, I make a decision, create a plan of action, and follow through. That's what leaders are supposed to do.

I'll give you an example from my experience of how this played out. In the run-up to the 2016 presidential election, I was approached by a political group asking me to become a third-party candidate to run for president. It really took me by surprise, but it also appealed to me. So I took about two weeks to really consider it.

Here's how I *felt*. Like many people, I was frustrated with Washington. I was tired of the partisan politics and the fighting. I was frustrated that political leaders no longer communicated or worked with one another. And I could not support either Hillary Clinton or Donald Trump.

I also *knew* that many other voters felt the way I did, about Washington politics and the candidates. I knew I would be able to communicate with people and work with them to create positive compromises. But I also knew it was relatively late in the game to start a run for office. And I knew that a third-party candidate had never won a presidential election.

As much as I wanted to serve the country and work to change the sense of division and hostility in the United States, I *thought* I could never be anything other than a spoiler who took away votes from the other candidates but could not win. So I decided that what I *should do*, is pass.

DISCUSS

Answer the following questions and discuss your answers when you meet with your team.

1 What creates intuition?

_____

_____

_____

_____

2 Do you agree with the statement that intuition is not only natural but can also be developed? Explain.

_____

_____

_____

_____

3 What is a recent situation in which leadership intuition affected your organization?

_____

_____

_____

4 Which presents the biggest challenge for you: accurately reading your situation, trends, your resources, other people, or yourself? How can you improve your intuition in this area?

_____

_____

_____

_____

_____

_____

5 How well attuned are you to reading what you feel, what you know, and what you think? How does your awareness of this impact your confidence for what you should do? How can you improve by connecting these four areas?

_____

_____

_____

_____

_____

_____

APPLY

1 Have you trusted your intuition in the past? Make a list of important past leadership decisions that you've made. Next to each decision, put a plus or a minus indicating whether the outcome was more positive or negative. Then try to identify what you based the decision on. This will show you your intuitive track record. Look for patterns, both positive and negative.

_____

_____

_____

_____

_____

2 Do some work to become better at trusting your intuition. Start by using the four questions from this lesson:

- What do I feel?
- What do I know?
- What do I think?
- What should I do?

Remember to weigh how much you rely on each of the first three questions based on your natural gifting. Once you start using the questions, track how successful you are at making intuition-based decisions so that you can keep improving.

3 One of the most important abilities in leadership is reading people. How would you rate yourself in this area? Can you tell what others are feeling? Can you sense when people are upset? Happy? Confused? Angry? Do you anticipate what others are thinking? If this is not an area of strength for you, then read books on relationships, engage more people in conversations, and become a people watcher.

_____

_____

_____

_____

_____

_____

TAKE ACTION

How you see your world around you is determined by who you are. And while most people will just be accepting of situations, the intuitive leader looks at every situation and asks questions: Why is it this way? Why is it the popular choice? Why does it or why doesn't it work? What other ways could the situation be approached or the problem be solved? The intuitive leader observes and assesses.

Explore a leadership situation that either you or someone else is in where the decisions being made just don't seem right to you. It could be a situation in which you are the leader and everyone around you is telling you things are fine, but you still have some hesitations. Or it could be a situation in which you think another leader handled a situation incorrectly. Look at different ways the situation could be approached by answering the following questions:

1. What is the situation?
2. What is the popular choice? Why?
3. Why does it or doesn't it work?
4. What is your leadership intuition telling you?
5. What leadership law might it be violating?
6. Is the job being done as well as it could be?
7. Is what's being done damaging relationships?
8. What other way could the situation be approached or the problem be solved?

9

THE LAW OF MAGNETISM

Who You Are Is Who You Attract

You've probably heard the saying, "Birds of a feather flock together." And maybe you've found this to be true. When you were in school, you might have recognized that good students spent time with other good students, athletes spent time with other athletes, and those who only want to play stuck with those who were like-minded. Well, this idea is also true when it comes to leadership. Who makes up your team is less determined by what you want but more by who you are. In order to build a strong team, you must understand the Law of Magnetism.

READ

Someone who used the Law of Magnetism to be successful is Angela Ahrendts, the former senior vice president of retail at Apple and CEO of Burberry. In 2006, when Ahrendts accepted the job at Burberry, she left a job she loved as an executive vice president at fashion company Liz Claiborne. The main reason she left was because she wanted a chance to work with a luxury brand.[1] But Burberry was a brand that was in trouble.

The organization had a long history. Founded in 1856 by Thomas Burberry, the company took off when he invented gabardine, a breathable weatherproof fabric that revolutionized rainwear. After outfitting explorers such as Roald Amundsen and Earnest Shackleton, the reputation of Burberry's patented gabardine took off. The coats made of the fabric were so hard-wearing and useful that the British army gave Burberry a contract to manufacture them during World War I. Those coats came to be known as trench coats.[2] Humphrey Bogart wore a Burberry trench coat in *Casablanca*, and forms of that coat are still in style today.

But despite Burberry's notoriety and success, and the reception of two royal warrants, the company was no longer a respected brand. Where they once produced high-end apparel, for years Burberry had sold their name through dozens of licenses to manufacturers around the world who produced all manner of nonluxury products, including doggy diapers with Burberry's patented and once-revered plaid design.

Ahrendts was determined to turn Burberry around and make it not only respected again but also appealing to younger buyers. She also wanted to make it the largest luxury fashion brand in the world. Fortunately, already working at Burberry was a designer she had worked with and greatly respected: Christopher Bailey. She partnered with him to set Burberry in a new direction. "We really reconnected and we actually put the strategy together on the back of a napkin," said Ahrendts.[3] She saw a clear way forward: "We would reinforce our heritage, our Britishness, by emphasizing and growing our core luxury products, innovating them and keeping them at the heart of everything we did."[4]

Because Ahrendts was now leading a large staff whom she had not herself attracted, she needed to work to get everyone on board. "I have to admit that some managers were cynical. A lot of them had been at Burberry for a really long time."[5] So she came up with a solution:

> Maybe six months in, we had had a huge offsite [meeting], and we had 200 of the top executives from around the world we flew in.
>
> And I'm a pretty good read of people. My right brain kicks in and I'm just watching. And this was two or three days. And at the very end I got up and I said, "Look, this is the strategy. This is what we're doing. And I know some of you are skeptical and I know you've been here for a long time and I know the way you think you're doing it in Hong Kong or Korea is the best, but it's not. We won't win. We're not winning now and you're not, right?"
>
> And I said, "So, I am happy to meet with you after this meeting and give you the greatest retirement package. I'm not looking to hurt anybody, but you need to walk out of here 100% believing in everything we're doing—or I don't want you on the team and I will take care of you. But we can't afford it. We have no time."[6]

Another significant thing she did was facilitate changes to Burberry's board. Most of its members were older, and since Ahrendts wanted the brand to become more tech savvy and to appeal to younger customers, especially millennials, she put younger people on the board and asked the older members who were stepping off to mentor them. The move struck a great balance between attracting and empowering people more like herself while harnessing the wisdom and experience of those who served the company before her. And she hired younger staff. In 2013, she noted that most of the employees at their corporate headquarters in London were under thirty.[7]

In 2014, Ahrendts left the company to work for Apple. In the eight years Ahrendts led Burberry as its CEO, the company's stock price doubled. So did revenue and operating income. According to Interbrand, Burberry was the fastest growing luxury brand and the fourth-fastest growing brand globally, behind Apple, Google, and Amazon.[8]

OBSERVE

Once you understand the Law of Magnetism, you can see it at work in just about any kind of situation: business, government, sports, education, the military, and more. And once you embrace it, you can use it to improve your team and organization.

1 What challenges did Angela Ahrendts face when she became CEO of Burberry?

_____

_____

_____

_____

_____

2 What are some steps that she took to overcome those challenges?

_____

_____

_____

_____

_____

3 Do you agree with the idea that the team is often an extension of the leader's personality? Give an example that supports your answer.

_____

_____

_____

_____

4 What is an example from your own industry or area of service that illustrates how leaders tend to attract people who are like themselves?

_____

_____

_____

_____

LEARN

Maybe you've started thinking about the people that you have attracted in your organization. You might say to yourself, *Wait a minute. I can name twenty things that make the people I lead different from me.* And my response would be, "Of course, you can." We're all individuals. But the people who are drawn to you probably have more similarities than differences, especially in a few key areas.

GENERATION

Most organizations reflect the characteristics of their key leaders, and that includes their age. During the dot-com boom of the 1990s, thousands of companies were founded by people in their twenties and early thirties. And who did they hire? Others in their twenties and thirties. In just about any type of organization, much of the time the people who come on board are similar in age to the leaders who hire them.

ATTITUDE

Rarely have I seen positive and negative people attracted to one another. People who view life as a series of opportunities and exciting challenges don't want to hear others complain about how bad things are all the time. Attitude is one of the most contagious qualities a human being possesses. People with good attitudes tend to make people around them feel more positive. Those with a terrible attitude tend to bring others down.

BACKGROUND

In the lesson on the Law of Process, I wrote about Theodore Roosevelt. One of his memorable accomplishments was his daring charge up San Juan Hill with the Rough Riders during the Spanish-American War. Roosevelt personally recruited that all-volunteer cavalry company, and it was said to be a remarkably peculiar group of people. It was comprised primarily of two types of men: wealthy aristocrats from the Northeast and cowboys from the Wild West. Why? Because TR was an aristocratic-born, Harvard-educated New Yorker who turned himself into a real-life cowboy and big-game hunter in the Dakotas of the West. He was a strong and genuine leader in both worlds, and as a result, he attracted both kinds of people.

People attract—and are attracted to—others of similar background. Blue-collar workers tend to stick together. People with education tend to respect and value others who are also well educated. And to be blunt, people tend to hire employees of the same race unless they make an intentional effort to break that pattern. That's why the NFL introduced the Rooney Rule, which requires teams to interview at least one minority candidate for every head coaching position. This natural magnetism is so strong that organizations that value diversity have to fight against it.

VALUES

People are attracted to leaders whose values are similar to theirs. Think about the people who flocked to President John F. Kennedy after he was elected in 1960. He was a young idealist who wanted to change the world, and he attracted people with a similar profile. When he formed the Peace Corps and called people to service, saying, "Ask not what your country can do for you; ask what you can do for your country," thousands of young, idealistic people stepped forward to answer the challenge.

The law of magnetism is in effect whether the shared values are positive or negative. Think about someone like Adolf Hitler. He was a strong leader (as you can judge by his level of influence), but his values were rotten to the core. What kinds of people did he attract? Leaders with similar values: Joseph Goebbels, a bitter anti-Semite who ran Hitler's propaganda machine; Reinhard Heydrich, second in command of the Nazi secret police, who ordered mass executions of Nazi opponents; and Heinrich Himmler, chief of the SS and director of the Gestapo who initiated the systematic execution of Jews. They were all strong leaders, and they were all utterly evil men. The Law of Magnetism is powerful. Whatever character you possess is what you will likely find in the people who follow you.

ENERGY

It's a good thing that people with similar levels of energy are attracted to one another, because when you pair a high-energy person with a low-energy person and ask them to work closely together, they can drive one another crazy. The high-energy person thinks the low-energy one is lazy, and the low-energy person thinks the high-energy one is out of control.

GIFTEDNESS

People are most likely to respect and follow someone who possesses their kind of talent. Businesspeople want to follow leaders with skill in building an organization and making a profit. Football players want to follow coaches who can win championships. Creative people want to follow other creatives who are willing to think outside the box. Like attracts like.

LEADERSHIP ABILITY

Finally, the people you attract will have leadership ability similar to your own. As I said in discussing the Law of Respect, people naturally follow leaders *stronger* than themselves. But you also have to factor in the Law of Magnetism, which states that who you are is who you attract. If you are a 7 when it comes to leadership, you are more likely to draw 5s and 6s to you than 2s and 3s. The leaders you attract will be similar in style and ability to you.

Answer the following questions and discuss your answers when you meet with your team.

1 How have these six common-ground areas played a part in the makeup and growth of your organization?

_____

_____

_____

_____

_____

2 Which of these common-ground areas has the strongest draw in deciding whom you
   follow? Explain.

   _____

   _____

   _____

   _____

   _____

3 Which of these common-ground areas do you find attracts the most people to you?
   Give an example.

   _____

   _____

   _____

   _____

   _____

   _____

4 How has your ability to attract others positively or negatively affected your leadership?

   _____

   _____

   _____

   _____

   _____

5 How can you work to become a more magnetic leader?

   _____

   _____

   _____

   _____

   _____

APPLY

1 Based on who you are attracting, you may need to grow in the areas of character and leadership. Find mentors willing and able to help you grow in each area. Good candidates as a character mentor could be a pastor or spiritual advisor, a professional whose ability you respect, or a professional coach. Ideally, your leadership mentor should work in the same or a similar profession and be several steps ahead of you in his or her career.

_____

_____

_____

_____

_____

_____

_____

_____

_____

_____

2 If you're not attracting the caliber of team member you desire, you may need to grow in the areas of character and leadership. Find mentors willing and able to help you grow in each area. Possible character mentors could include a pastor, spiritual advisor, or professional coach. Ideally, your leadership mentor would work in the same or a similar profession and be several steps ahead of you in his or her career.

_____

_____

_____

_____

_____

_____

_____

_____

3 If you are already attracting the kinds of people you desire, then it's time to take your leadership to the next level. Work at staffing your weaknesses and recruiting people who will complement your leadership. Write a list of your five greatest strengths. Then write your five greatest weaknesses. Now create a profile of who you are looking for. Start with a list of strengths and natural gifts that would compensate for your weaknesses. Add to that values and attitude similar to yours. Also consider the benefits of seeking someone different in age, background, education, and race. Keep in mind that whoever you choose must possess leadership potential or at the very least an understanding of, and appreciation for, leadership.

_____

_____

_____

_____

TAKE ACTION

Effective leaders are always on the lookout for good people. I think each of us carries around a mental list of what kind of people we would like to have in our organization or department. Think about it. Do you know who you're looking for right now? What is your profile of perfect employees? What qualities would they possess? Would you want them to be aggressive and entrepreneurial? Kind and compassionate? Technically savvy? Highly relational? Stop right now, take a moment, and make a list of the qualities you'd like in the people on your team.

My people would have these qualities:

_____

_____

_____

_____

_____

_____

_____

Go back to the list you just made, and for each characteristic you identified, decide whether you possess that quality. For example, if you wrote that you would like "great leaders" and you are an excellent leader, that's a match. Put a check (✓) by it. But if your leadership is no better than average, put an X and write "only average leader" next to it. If you wrote that you want people who are "entrepreneurial" and you possess that quality, put a check. Otherwise, mark it with an X, and so on. Now review the whole list.

If you see a whole bunch of Xs, then you're in trouble, because the people you describe are not the type who will want to follow you. In most situations, unless you take strong measures to counteract it, you will draw people to you who possess the same qualities you do. So, think about what you can do to possess the qualities on your list that you marked with an X. Who can you learn this from? What resources would help you? Create a plan to improve yourself.

10

THE LAW OF CONNECTION

Leaders Touch a Heart Before
They Ask for a Hand

For leaders to be effective, they must connect with people. Why? If you want to lead well, you must touch people's hearts before you ask them for a hand. That is the Law of Connection. All great leaders and communicators recognize this truth and act on it almost instinctively. You can't move people to action unless you first move them with emotion.

READ

Never underestimate the power of making connections and building relationships with people before asking them to follow you. If you've ever studied the lives of notable military commanders, you have probably noticed that the best ones practiced the Law of Connection. I read that during World War I in France, General Douglas MacArthur told a battalion commander before a daring charge, "Major, when the signal comes to go over the top, I want you to go first, before your men. If you do, they'll follow." Then MacArthur removed the Distinguished Service Cross from his own uniform and pinned it on the major. He had, in effect, awarded him for heroism before asking him to exhibit it. And of course, the major led his men, they followed him over the top, and they achieved their objective.

Not all military examples of the Law of Connection are quite so dramatic, but they are still effective. For example, it's said that Napoleon made it a practice to know every one of his officers by name and to remember where they lived and which battles they had fought with him. More recently, General Norman Schwarzkopf, leader of US Central Command during Operation Desert Storm, connected with his troops during the Gulf War. On Christmas in 1990, he spent the day in the mess halls among the men and women who were so far away from their families. In his autobiography, he said:

> I shook hands with everyone in the line, went behind the serving counter to greet the cooks and helpers, and worked my way through the mess hall, hitting every table, wishing everyone Merry Christmas. Then I went into the second and third dining facilities and did the same thing. I came back to the first mess tent and repeated the exercise, because by this time there was an entirely new set of faces. Then I sat down with some of the troops and had my dinner. In the course of four hours, I must have shaken four thousand hands.[1]

Schwarzkopf was a general. Did he have to do that? No, but he did. He used one of the most effective methods for connecting with others, something I call walking slowly through the crowd. By doing that, he let his service members know that he believed in them, he set the example for them, and he valued them.

As a leader, do the same. Go where your people are. Make yourself available to them. Learn people's names. Tell them how much you appreciate them. Find out how they're doing. And most important, listen. Leaders who relate to their people and really connect with them are leaders that people will follow to the ends of the earth.

OBSERVE

Good leaders work at connecting with others all the time, whether they are communicating to an entire organization or working with a single individual. The stronger the relationship you form with followers, the greater the connection you forge—and the more likely those followers will want to help you. I used to tell my staff, "People don't care how much you know until they know how much you care." They would groan because they heard me say it so many times, but they recognized the truth of it nonetheless. You develop credibility with people when you connect with them and show that you genuinely care and want to help them. And as a result, they usually respond in kind and want to help you.

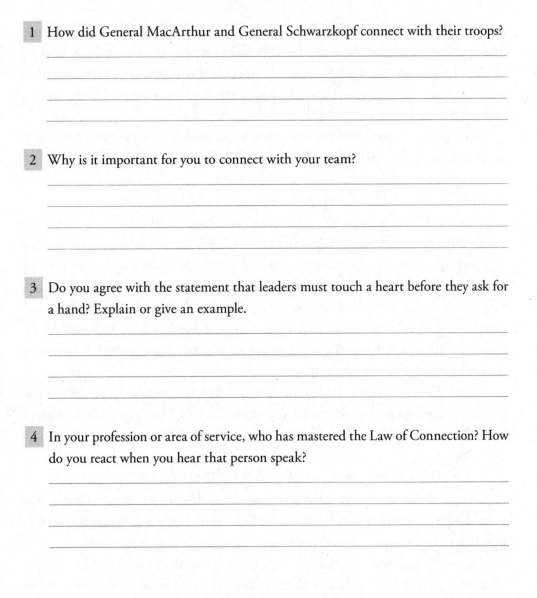

1　How did General MacArthur and General Schwarzkopf connect with their troops?

_____

_____

_____

_____

2　Why is it important for you to connect with your team?

_____

_____

_____

_____

3　Do you agree with the statement that leaders must touch a heart before they ask for a hand? Explain or give an example.

_____

_____

_____

_____

4　In your profession or area of service, who has mastered the Law of Connection? How do you react when you hear that person speak?

_____

_____

_____

_____

LEARN

One key to connecting with others is recognizing that even in a group, you have to relate to people as individuals. I've had the opportunity to speak to some wonderful audiences during the course of my career. The largest have been in stadiums with more than sixty thousand people in attendance. People ask me, "How in the world do you communicate with that many people?" The secret is simple. I don't try to talk to the thousands. I focus on talking to one person. That's the only way to connect with people. It's the same way when writing a book. I don't think of the millions of people who have read my books. I think of one person: *you*. I believe that if I can connect with you as an individual, then what I have to offer might be able to help you. If I'm not connecting, you'll stop reading and go do something else.

How do you connect? Whether you're speaking in front of a large audience or chatting in the hallway with an individual, there are three things you need to keep in mind:

WHAT PEOPLE NEED TO KNOW: YOU BELIEVE IN THEM

One of the most precious gifts a leader can give people is belief in them. Too many have a difficult time finding their way in life. They've never had someone who truly believes in them and speaks into their lives. They don't know their own strengths and weaknesses. They are uncertain about the future. Leaders who connect help people believe in themselves and in the work they're doing. But that doesn't mean giving insincere compliments. People can smell a phony a mile away. Legendary NFL coach Bill Walsh observed, "Nothing is more effective than sincere, accurate praise, and nothing is more lame than a cookie-cutter compliment."

French general Napoleon Bonaparte said, "A leader is a dealer in hope." When you genuinely believe in people and can communicate that belief, you give them hope and a better future.

WHAT PEOPLE NEED TO SEE: YOU WILL BE AN EXAMPLE

Perhaps the most impacting thing you can do as a leader and communicator is to practice what you preach. That's where credibility comes from. Modeling good values demonstrates trustworthiness and consistency—and consistency compounds.

Plenty of people say one thing but do something else. People with that kind of "do what I say, not what I do" attitude don't last as leaders because people don't want to follow people who lack integrity. Authenticity connects with people.

WHAT PEOPLE NEED TO FEEL: YOU VALUE THEM

In the end, your greatest asset for connecting with people is caring for them. People can tell when you genuinely care about them and value them as individuals, and it draws them to you. I learned this as a child from one of my teachers, Miss Tacey. Once when I got sick, she came to visit me at home to see how I was doing, and to tell me how much she missed having me in class. You can bet I couldn't wait to get well and get back.

As a leader, you cannot value people and add value to them if you do not care about them or secretly resent them. You must develop genuine respect for them and place value on them, not for what they can do for you, but simply because they have value as human beings. Do that, and you will be able to connect with them.

There's one more point I need to make about connecting with people: it's the leader's job, not the follower's. Some leaders have problems with the Law of Connection because they put the responsibility for connecting on the people they lead. That is especially true of positional leaders. They often think, *I'm the boss. These are my employees. Let them come to me.* But successful leaders who obey the Law of Connection are always initiators. They take the first step with others and then make the effort to continue building relationships. That's not always easy, but it's important to the success of the organization. A leader has to do it, no matter how many obstacles there might be.

THE RESULT OF CONNECTION

When a leader truly has done the work to connect with his people, you can see it in the way the organization functions. Employees exhibit loyalty and a strong work ethic. The vision of the leader becomes the aspiration of the people. The impact is incredible.

One of the companies I admire is Southwest Airlines, a pioneer in budget airlines and now the largest domestic airline in the United States. The company has been successful and profitable while other airlines have filed for bankruptcy and folded. The person responsible for the initial success of the organization and the creation of its culture is Herb Kelleher, the company's founder.

I love what Southwest's employees did on Boss's Day in 1994 because it shows the kind of connection Kelleher made with his people. They took out a full-page ad in *USA Today* and addressed the following message to Kelleher:

Thanks, Herb
For remembering every one of our names.
For supporting the Ronald McDonald House.

For helping load baggage on Thanksgiving.

For giving everyone a kiss (and we mean everyone).

For listening.

For running the only profitable major airline.

For singing at our holiday party.

For singing only once a year.

For letting us wear shorts and sneakers to work.

For golfing at The LUV Classic with only one club.

For outtalking Sam Donaldson.

For riding your Harley Davidson into Southwest Headquarters.

For being a friend, not just a boss.

Happy Boss's Day from Each One of Your 16,000 Employees3

A display of affection like that occurs only when a leader has worked hard to connect with his people.

Don't ever underestimate the importance of building relational bridges between yourself and the people you lead. There's an old saying: to lead yourself, use your head; to lead others, use your heart. That's the nature of the Law of Connection. Always touch a person's heart before you ask for a hand.

DISCUSS

Answer the following questions and discuss your answers when you meet with your team.

1 How does the ability to connect with others relate to leadership?

_____

_____

_____

2 How long does it normally take you to connect with someone? Explain.

_____

_____

_____

3 Which of the three keys to connection do you do best? Which is an area of weakness?

_____

_____

_____

_____

_____

4 Do you agree with the statement that it is the leader's job, not the follower's, to be the initiator of connection? Why or why not?

_____

_____

_____

_____

_____

5 How have you connected recently with someone on your team? Did you initiate the relationship or did that person initiate it? Up to now, why did you think it was or wasn't important to connect with people in your work environment?

_____

_____

_____

_____

_____

6 How can you initiate more healthy work relationships?

_____

_____

_____

_____

APPLY

1 How dedicated are you to believing in people, being a positive example to them, and genuinely valuing them? How would the people you lead assess you in these three areas? If you could stand to improve, examine your motives for leading. If your desire to help people and improve the team is overshadowed by personal ambition or selfishness, your ability to connect with people will suffer. Change your mind-set and your attitude so that you can become a better leader.

_____

_____

_____

_____

2 Learn to walk slowly through the crowd. When you are out among your employees or coworkers, make relationship building and connecting a priority. Before talking about work matters, make a connection. With people you don't yet know, that may take some time. With people you know well, still take a moment to connect relationally. It may cost you only a few minutes a day, but it will pay huge dividends in the future. And it will make the workplace a more positive environment.

_____

_____

_____

_____

3 Good leaders are good communicators. On a scale of 1 to 10, how would you rate yourself as a public speaker? If you give yourself anything lower than an 8, you need to work on improving your skills. Read books on communication, take a class, become a certified speaker, or join Toastmasters. Then sharpen your skills by practicing teaching and communicating. If you don't have opportunities to do that on the job, then try volunteering.

_____

_____

_____

_____

TAKE ACTION

When a leader has done the work to connect with his people, you can see it in the way the organization functions. Among employees there is incredible loyalty and a strong work ethic. The vision of the leader becomes the aspiration of the people, and the impact is incredible.

This week, spend time connecting with someone on your team that you don't already know very well. Find an appropriate situation that will allow you to talk about interests outside of work. You could ask the person to join you or a group for lunch. If that's not an option, look to see if the person has anything in their workspace that might be a conversation starter (pictures of family, college memorabilia, collectables or souvenirs in plain sight). Make it a goal to learn three things about the person.

11

THE LAW OF THE INNER CIRCLE

Those Closest to You Determine the Level of Your Success

When we see incredibly gifted people, we can be tempted to believe that talent alone made them successful. To think that is to buy into a lie. Nobody does anything great alone. Leaders do not succeed alone. Those closest to them determine the level of their success. What makes the difference is the leader's inner circle.

READ

I've been very fortunate, because I've had a fantastic inner circle that has made me a better leader and helped me accomplish more than I ever could on my own. It started with my parents when I was a kid. I married well. Margaret faithfully supports me and loves me unconditionally in spite of my quirks and shortcomings. My brother Larry, a fantastic entrepreneur, advises me on business matters. I've had advisors and mentors who have helped me and shaped me. And I've been aided by people who compensate for my weaknesses and bring skills to the table that I lack.

The people in my inner circle have changed over the years, with some people leaving and others arriving to help me. For example, when I was in my mid-thirties, Barbara Brumagin came alongside me and made me better. She was my executive assistant for eleven years. After she moved away to take a leadership position, Linda Eggers, who

111

was already working with me, became my executive assistant. She still serves me in that capacity today more than thirty-five years later. She is indispensable to me, not only in handling the details of my life, but because she knows how I think and answers others in my place. Over 90 percent of the time she doesn't even need to consult me.

I tell leaders all the time, the first and most important hiring decision executives can make is who they will choose as their assistant. If you have a good one in your inner circle, it improves your leadership significantly. He or she will save you time, help your life to run more smoothly, and enable you to remain focused on what only you can do. A good assistant should be in the room with you for every important meeting. When Linda accompanies me, I don't have to carry anything into the meeting or out of it after we're done.

Another longtime member of my inner circle is Charlie Wetzel, my writing partner. I hired him as my researcher, but in the first months he worked with me he proved his value when he reworked the manuscript of *Developing the Leaders Around You* at the request of my publisher. That first year he helped me write three books, as well as articles, product descriptions, and marketing pieces. It wasn't long before I wanted him in the room any time we were discussing writing or publishing. Charlie has been with me for twenty-eight years and together we've produced more than a hundred books.

The third longtime member of my inner circle is Mark Cole. I wasn't even the person who hired Mark. He was hired by someone in one of my companies and worked in the stock room and then in sales. As he rose in responsibility, I got to know him better. By the time he became a vice president, he become a confidant. When he proved himself, he became the CEO of all four of my organizations. Today, he's not only the CEO but also a co-owner of the companies and my successor. No one serves me or helps me the way Mark does and has for twenty years.

Leaders are hired to deliver results. There is no substitute for performance. But without a good team, they often don't get the opportunity. Those closest to them determine the level of their success. That is the Law of the Inner Circle.

OBSERVE

Leadership expert Warren Bennis was right when he maintained, "The leader finds greatness in the group, and he or she helps the members find it in themselves."[1] Think of any highly effective leader, and you will find someone who surrounded himself with a strong inner circle. You can see it in business, ministry, sports, and even family relationships. Those closest to you determine the level of your success.

1   What does the longevity of someone's inner circle say about their leadership?

_____

_____

_____

2   To what do you attribute the formation and longevity of a leader's inner circle? How much of it is luck? How much is due to circumstances? How much to their profession? How much to character? To competence?

_____

_____

_____

_____

3   Think of someone in your profession or area of service whom you consider successful. How has that person utilized the Law of the Inner Circle?

_____

_____

_____

_____

4   How will your potential be affected if you don't form a strong inner circle?

_____

_____

_____

LEARN

Most human beings have some kind of inner circle—people close to them who help to make or break them. However, many people are not strategic in choosing them. Few people give enough thought to how those closest to them impact their effectiveness or leadership potential. We naturally tend to surround ourselves with either people we like or people with whom we are comfortable. But people who bring nothing more than fun or easiness will not help you to be successful. You see it all the time with certain athletes who transition to the professional ranks and with entertainers who achieve professional success. Some plateau or self-destruct because their inner circle is composed of people who are not helpful or are even harmful to them.

To practice the Law of the Inner Circle, you must be *intentional* in your relationship building. You need to invest in the best people around you and see how they respond. As you look for potential inner circle members, take the advice of longtime executive and retired president, CEO, and chairman of Agilent Technologies, Ned Barnholt. He believes there are three kinds of people in an organization when it comes to leadership: (1) those who get it almost immediately and they're off and running with it; (2) those who are skeptical and not sure what to do with it; and (3) another third who start out negative and hope it will go away. "I used to spend most of my time with those who were the most negative," says Barnholt, "trying to convince them to change. Now I spend my time with the people in the first [group]. I'm investing in my best assets."[2]

As people rise up, think about these three pre-qualifications before you begin drawing them in closer to become inner circle members. Only if they are solid in these three areas should you bring them into your circle.

1. WHO THEY ARE

Anyone who is going to be an integral part of your life needs to have good character and share the same values you have. When I invite people onto my team or consider them for my inner circle, I expect them to:

- **Have Integrity:** They need to be honest and truthful and do what they say they'll do.
- **Possess a Positive Attitude:** A negative attitude never led anyone to a positive solution.
- **Value Excellence:** Nothing hurts a business or a team more than settling for average.
- **Show Flexibility:** I want to be able to change on a dime to pursue new opportunities or improve on something we're already doing.

- **Exhibit Loyalty:** We all need to work together toward a common cause and respect one another as we do.
- **Value People:** Anyone who works with me must care about people and treat them with respect and dignity.

I could go on, but I'm sure you get the idea. I will say this. In the past when I haven't paid close enough attention to the values of someone I brought into my inner circle, I regretted it. So make sure to come up with your own list of values and then make sure a potential inner-circle member possesses those values.

2. What They Do

Every person in my inner circle is fantastic at what they do. If they weren't, they wouldn't be there. They make me, the team, and the organization better because of their skills, talents, and ability.

Because of my leadership giftedness, I naturally attract leaders. However, one of the best things I have done in my leadership career is to bring people into my inner circle who possess strengths that I don't. Because of this, they can point out my blind spots, compensate for my weaknesses, push back with perspectives different from my own, and bring different strengths to the organization. It's a great win-win.

I'm a big believer in team chemistry. If your inner circle is going to work together and function as a team, then you need to consider how members interact with each other, how they fit. Just as members of a championship basketball team have complementary skills and compatible roles, you want all inner circle members to have places where they contribute. And they should make one another better, raise one another's game, whether by sharing information and wisdom or engaging in friendly competition. When they improve one another, they also improve your entire team.

3. How They Lessen My Load

I discussed in the Law of Addition how people add, subtract, multiply, or divide when it comes to others. The people in your inner circle must be adders or multipliers. They should have a proven track record as assets to the organization. And they should take some of the leadership load off you.

When I was growing up, my mother used to recite a poem to me by Ella Wheeler Wilcox. I've never forgotten it:

There are two kinds of people on earth to-day,

Just two kinds of people; no more, I say.

Not the sinner and saint, for it's well understood,

The good are half bad, and the bad are half good. . . .

No; the two kinds of people on earth I mean,

Are the people who lift and the people who lean.[3]

Your inner circle members need to be lifters, not just professionally, but also to you personally. They should add value to you. That may sound selfish, but it's not. Only if you reach your potential as a leader will the people on your team or in your organization have a chance to reach their potential. If the people around you don't make you better, then you need to get around other people.

I'll mention one other factor to consider when thinking about potential inner circle members. Some people naturally belong in your inner circle because of their importance to the organization. For example, by virtue of being my CEO, Mark Cole should be in my inner circle because my organizations cannot function without his leadership. However, Mark didn't become an inner circle member because of his position. Because he exhibits the three characteristics I already described, he became a member of my inner circle, and from there he earned the right to become my CEO. If people are in your inner circle due only to their position and you wouldn't otherwise put them there, then you may need to start looking for someone else to fill the position.

DISCUSS

Answer the following questions and discuss your answers when you meet with your team.

1 Do you agree with this list of three pre-qualifications when it comes to creating your inner circle? What other qualities would you look for?

_____

_____

_____

_____

2 In the past, how have you selected people for your inner circle?

_____

_____

_____

_____

3 What are common characteristics found in the people with whom you surround yourself?

_____

_____

_____

_____

4 Have the people you've chosen to be in your inner circle enhanced your life or made it more difficult? If they've done more harm than good, how do you need to change your selection process?

_____

_____

_____

_____

APPLY

1 Who is in your inner circle? List their names and next to each write how that person contributes to you and what they're working to accomplish. If they do not have a clear role or function, then write how you believe they have *the potential* to contribute. Look for holes and duplications. Then begin looking for people to fill the gaps.

_____

_____

_____

_____

2   Great inner circles do not come together by accident. Effective leaders are continually developing current and future inner circle members. How do they do it?

- They spend extra time with them strategically to mentor them and to develop relationships.
- They give them extra responsibility and place higher expectations on them.
- They give them more credit when things go well and hold them accountable when they don't.

Examine your list of inner circle members to determine whether you are taking these steps with them. If not, make changes. In addition, be sure to use this development strategy with a pool of new potential inner circle members.

3   If you have already developed an inner circle and it is functioning well, then start looking for individuals to help you in your outer circle. Search for people who challenge you and spark your creativity. As your guide, remember the words of Solomon of ancient Israel, who wrote, "As iron sharpens iron, friends sharpen the minds of each other."[4]

_____

_____

_____

_____

_____

_____

_____

TAKE ACTION

List the names of three current inner circle members. Next to each name, explain why that person is a part of your inner circle. What qualities and skills does he or she bring to the table? How does that person's abilities compliment and complete your abilities? How does he or she support you emotionally? How does that person move you closer to your goals for the team?

Inner circle member: _____

Contributions:

_____

_____

_____

_____

_____

Inner circle member: _____

Contributions:

_____

_____

_____

_____

_____

Inner circle member: _____

Contributions:

_____

_____

_____

_____

_____

If there are people on your list who add no value or who bring you down, you should consider moving them out of your inner circle. Next, try to identify three more people whom you might want to add to your inner circle. Next to each person's name, list the unique skills and qualities that he or she would bring to the group. Look for people who can fill a need that is not already being filled by another member of your inner circle. Remember that your inner circle should be made up of people from different areas of your life so you can receive a well-rounded balance of feedback and insight.

Potential inner circle member: _____

Potential contributions:

_____
_____
_____
_____
_____

Potential inner circle member: _____

Potential contributions:

_____
_____
_____
_____
_____

Potential inner circle member: _____

Potential contributions:

_____
_____
_____
_____

12

◆◆◆

THE LAW OF EMPOWERMENT

Only Secure Leaders Give
Power to Others

The greatest enemy of empowerment is the fear of losing what we have. Many leaders worry that if they help subordinates, they themselves will become dispensable. But the truth is that the only way to make yourself *indispensable* is to raise up leaders. If you are able to continually empower others and help them develop so that they become capable of taking over your job, you will become so valuable to the organization that you become indispensable. That's a paradox of the Law of Empowerment.

READ

Nearly everyone has heard of Henry Ford, the revolutionary automobile industry innovator and legend in American business history. In 1903, he cofounded the Ford Motor Company with the belief that the future of the automobile lay in putting it within the reach of the average American worker. Ford said,

> I will build a motorcar for the multitude. It will be large enough for the family but small enough for the individual to run and care for. It will be constructed of the best materials, by the best men to be hired, after the simplest designs that modern engineering can devise. But it will be so low in price that no man making a good salary will be unable

to own one—and enjoy with his family the blessings of hours of pleasure in God's great open spaces.[1]

Henry Ford carried out that vision with the Model T, and it changed the face of twentieth-century American life. By 1914, Ford was producing nearly 50 percent of all automobiles in the United States. The Ford Motor Company looked like an American success story.

However, all of Ford's story is not about positive achievement, and one reason is that he didn't embrace the Law of Empowerment. He held on to power instead of empowering others. Ford was so in love with his Model T that he never wanted to change or improve it—nor did he want anyone else to tinker with it. One day when a group of his designers surprised him by presenting him with the prototype of an improved model, Ford furiously ripped its doors off the hinges and proceeded to destroy the car with his bare hands.

For almost twenty years, the Ford Motor Company offered only one design, the Model T, which Henry Ford had personally developed. It wasn't until 1927 that he finally—grudgingly—agreed to offer a new car to the public. The company finally produced the Model A, but it was incredibly far behind its competitors in technical innovations. Despite its early head start and the incredible lead over its competitors, the Ford Motor Company's market share kept shrinking. By 1931, it was down to only 28 percent, a little more than half of what it produced seventeen years earlier.

Henry Ford was the antithesis of an empowering leader. He continually undermined his leaders and looked over the shoulders of his people to control them. He even created a sociological department within Ford Motor Company to check up on his employees and direct their private lives.

Perhaps Ford's most peculiar dealings were with his executives, especially his son Edsel. The younger Ford had worked at the company since he was a boy. As Henry became more eccentric, Edsel worked harder to keep the company going. If it weren't for Edsel, the Ford Motor Company probably would have gone out of business in the 1930s. Henry eventually gave Edsel the presidency of the company, but at the same time he undermined him. Whenever any promising leader was rising up in the company, Henry tore him down, causing the company to lose its best executives. The few who stayed did so because they hoped to see Edsel finally take over and set things right. But Edsel died in 1943 at age forty-nine.

Edsel's oldest son, the twenty-six-year-old Henry Ford II, left the navy so that he could return to Dearborn, Michigan, and take over the company. At first, he faced opposition. But within two years, he gathered the support of several key people, received the backing of the board of directors (his mother controlled 41 percent of Ford Motor Company's stock), and convinced his grandfather to step down so that he could become president in his place.

Young Henry was taking over a company that hadn't made a profit in fifteen years and was losing $1 million *a day*! The young president knew he was in over his head, so he brought in high-level leaders such as Colonel Charles "Tex" Thornton, who led a team at the War Department during World War II; and Ernie Breech, an experienced General Motors executive and the former president of Bendix Aviation. By 1949, Ford Motor Company was on a roll again.

But there was too much of his grandfather in Henry Ford II. He felt threatened by these good leaders, so he pitted one executive against another. Anytime an executive gained power and influence, Henry undercut the person's authority by moving him to a position with less clout, supporting the executive's subordinates, or publicly humiliating him. This maneuver continued all the days Henry II was at Ford.[2] As one-time Ford president Lee Iacocca commented after leaving the company, "Henry Ford, as I would learn firsthand, had a nasty habit of getting rid of strong leaders." Iacocca said Henry Ford II once described his leadership philosophy to him: "If a guy works for you, don't let him get too comfortable. Don't let him get cozy or set in his ways. Always do the opposite of what he expects. Keep your people anxious and off-balance."[3]

The leadership of both Henry Fords violated the Law of Empowerment. Rather than building leaders up; giving them resources, authority, and responsibility; and then empowering them to achieve, they often undermined their best people. Their insecurity made it impossible for them to give power to others. Ultimately, it diminished their personal leadership potential, created havoc in the lives of the people around them, and damaged their organization.

OBSERVE

If leaders want to be successful, they have to be willing to empower others. I like the way President Theodore Roosevelt stated it: "The best executive is the one who has sense enough to pick good men to do what he wants done, and the self-restraint enough to keep from meddling with them while they do it."

1 Why did the Ford Company lose its market share?

_____

_____

_____

_____

_____

2 How did both Henry Ford and Henry Ford II violate the Law of Empowerment? How did this affect their company?

_____

_____

_____

_____

_____

3 Think of a leader in your profession or area of service who violated the Law of Empowerment. How did that affect the organization?

_____

_____

_____

_____

_____

4 Think of a leader in your profession or area of service who exemplified the Law of Empowerment. How did that affect the organization?

_____

_____

_____

_____

_____

LEARN

To lead others well, we must help them to reach their potential. That means being on their side, encouraging them, sharing the power we have with them, and helping them to succeed. That's not traditionally what we're taught about leadership. The two leadership games I was taught as a kid were King of the Hill and Follow the Leader. What was the object of King of the Hill? To knock other people down so that you can be on top. And what was the point in Follow the Leader? To do things you *knew* followers couldn't do to separate yourself from them and beat them. The problem with those games is that to win, you have to make everyone else lose. The games are based on insecurity and power, the opposite of the way to raise up leaders.

I believe people have a natural desire to gain power and hold on to it. Some do it to enrich themselves. Others desire to control other people to get what they want from them. Some people tell themselves they want power so that they can do good, but the moment they manipulate others or justify bad behavior to hold on to power, they begin doing harm, no matter how they justify it. Lord Acton stated, "Power tends to corrupt, and absolute power corrupts absolutely."[4] The recent #MeToo and Black Lives Matter movements are reactions against powerful people using their power to harm others with less power.

When I travel to developing countries, I am made especially aware of how alien the idea of empowerment can be to emerging leaders. In cultures where people need to fight to make something of themselves, the assumption is that they need to fight others to maintain their leadership. They put others down to lift themselves up. But that reflects a scarcity mind-set. The truth is that if you give some of your power away to others, there is still plenty to go around. Pushing people down takes you down with them. Lifting others up lifts you up.

BARRIERS TO EMPOWERMENT

Leading well is not about enriching yourself—it's about empowering others. Leadership analysts Lynne McFarland, Larry Senn, and John Childress affirm the "empowerment leadership model shifts away from 'position power' to 'people power,' within which all people are given leadership roles so they can contribute to their fullest capacity."[5] Only empowered people can reach their potential. When leaders can't or won't empower others, they create barriers within the organization that followers cannot overcome. If the barriers remain long enough, then the people give up and stop trying, or they go to another organization where they can maximize their potential.

If empowerment is so positive, then why don't more leaders do it? Many have never been taught how. But more often when leaders fail to empower others, it is usually due to one of these three reasons:

THE #1 BARRIER TO EMPOWERMENT: DESIRE FOR JOB SECURITY

The greatest enemy of empowerment is the fear of losing what we have. Many leaders worry that if they help subordinates, they themselves will become dispensable. But the truth is that the only way to make yourself *indispensable* is to raise up leaders. If you are able to continually empower others and help them develop so that they become capable of taking over your job, you will become so valuable to the organization that you become indispensable. That's a paradox of the Law of Empowerment.

What if I work myself out of a job by empowering others, you may ask, *and my superiors don't recognize my contribution?* That can happen in the short term. But if you keep raising up leaders and empowering them, you will develop a pattern of achievement, excellence, and leadership that will be recognized and rewarded. If the teams you lead always seem to succeed, people will figure out that you are leading them well.

THE #2 BARRIER TO EMPOWERMENT: RESISTANCE TO CHANGE

Nobel Prize–winning author John Steinbeck asserted, "It is the nature of man as he grows older . . . to protest against change, particularly change for the better."[6] By its very nature, empowerment brings constant change because it encourages people to grow and innovate. Change is the price of progress. That's not always easy to live with.

Most people don't like change, yet one of the most important responsibilities of leaders is to continually improve their organizations. As a leader, you must train yourself to embrace change, to desire it, to make a way for it. Effective leaders are not only willing to change; they become change agents.

THE #3 BARRIER TO EMPOWERMENT: LACK OF SELF-WORTH

Murphy's Twelfth Law states: "You can't lead a cavalry charge if you think you look funny on a horse."[7] Self-conscious people are rarely good leaders. They focus on themselves, worrying how they look, what others think, whether they are liked. They can't give power to others because they feel that they have no power themselves. And you can't give what you don't have.

Only secure leaders are able to give themselves away. Mark Twain once remarked that great things happen when you don't care who gets the credit. But I believe you can take that a step farther. I believe the greatest things happen *only* when you give others the credit. One-time vice-presidential candidate Admiral James B. Stockdale declared, "What we need for leaders are men [and women] of heart who are so helpful that they, in effect, do away with the need of their jobs. But leaders like that are never out of a job, never out of followers. Strange as it sounds, great leaders gain authority by giving it away."[8] If you aspire to be a great leader, you must live by the Law of Empowerment.

DISCUSS

Answer the following questions and discuss your answers when you meet with your team.

1 Why do you think that some leaders violate the Law of Empowerment?

_____

_____

_____

_____

2 Which of the three barriers to empowerment is most prevalent in your profession or area of service? Give examples.

_____

_____

_____

_____

3 How has a leader's resistance to the Law of Empowerment affected you and your teams in the past?

_____

_____

_____

4 How has a leader empowered you in the past? What was the result?

_____

_____

_____

_____

_____

5 Do you agree that the only way to become indispensable is to become dispensable? Explain.

_____

_____

_____

_____

_____

6 Are you more likely to resist empowering others due to your desire for job security, resistance to change, lack of self-worth, or another reason? How can you get past this leadership obstacle?

_____

_____

_____

_____

_____

7 What are some ways you will empower others in your current position?

_____

_____

_____

_____

_____

APPLY

1 How secure are you as a leader? Are you confident? Are you confident enough to train and empower others to take your place? If not, you will need to examine your self-worth and explore why you're hesitant to share your power with others.

_____

_____

_____

_____

2 How much do you believe in people? Make a list of the people who work for you. If there are too many to list, then write the names of your top three to five people. Now, rate each person's potential—not their current ability—on a scale of 1 to 10 (low to high). If the numbers are low, your belief in people isn't high enough, and you will have difficulty empowering others. Change your thinking by focusing on people's positive qualities and characteristics. Look for people's greatest strengths and envision how they can leverage those strengths to achieve significant things. Then help them do that.

_____

_____

_____

_____

3 Become an empowering leader. Use the five-step process to train and empower your best people. Take them with you, train them, coach them, and give them the responsibility and authority to succeed. Once you experience the joy and effectiveness of empowering others, you will have a hard time *not* giving your power away.

_____

_____

_____

_____

TAKE ACTION

One-time vice-presidential candidate Admiral James B. Stockdale declared, "What we need for leaders are men [and women] of heart who are so helpful that they, in effect, do away with the need of their jobs. But leaders like that are never out of a job, never out of followers. Strange as it sounds, great leaders gain authority by giving it away."[9]

This week, find one situation in which you can share your authority with someone else. It could be letting your child plan a family event for the weekend or giving someone on your team authority over a project. Answer the following questions throughout the week in order to evaluate the experience.

I shared my authority with _____
by empowering him or her to _____ .

1 Why did you choose to share your authority with this person?

_____

_____

_____

_____

_____

2 What were your initial concerns when sharing your authority with someone else?

_____

_____

_____

_____

_____

3 How did this person react to your offer?

_____

_____

_____

_____

_____

4 What were some of the challenges this person faced with the project, task, or decision?

_____

_____

_____

_____

_____

5 How did you encourage this person?

_____

_____

_____

_____

_____

6 How did you help the individual grow as a leader?

_____

_____

_____

_____

_____

7 What was the outcome of the project, task, or decision?

_____

_____

_____

_____

_____

8 How was sharing authority beneficial to you and to the other person?

_____

_____

_____

_____

_____

13

THE LAW OF THE PICTURE

People Do What People See

Good leaders are always conscious of the fact that they are setting the example and members of their team are going to do what they do, for better or worse. In general, the better the leaders' actions, the better their people's.

READ

In 2001, filmmaker Steven Spielberg and actor Tom Hanks produced a TV miniseries called *Band of Brothers* based on the book of the same name by historian Stephen Ambrose. The ten episodes chronicled the story of Easy Company, a group of paratroopers from the 101st Airborne who fought during World War II. The men of Easy Company were as tough as soldiers get, and they fought heroically from the invasion of Normandy to the end of the war.

The story of Easy Company is a great study in leadership, for the various officers and sergeants who commanded the men displayed leadership styles both good and bad. When the leadership was good, it made the difference, not only in the way the soldiers performed, but in the outcome of their battles and, ultimately, the war.

From the very first episode of the television series, the contrasting leadership styles were on display. Herbert Sobel, Easy Company's commanding officer during its training, was shown to be a brutal and autocratic leader with a sadistic streak. He drove the men harder than the commander of any other company. He arbitrarily revoked passes and inflicted punishment. But judging from Ambrose's research, Sobel was even worse than he was depicted in the series.

Sobel drove the men mercilessly, which was fine, since he was preparing them for combat. But he didn't push himself the same way, being *barely* capable of passing the physical test required of paratroopers. Nor did he display the high level of competence he demanded from everyone else. Ambrose wrote about an incident during training that was representative of Sobel's leadership:

> On one night exercise he [Sobel] decided to teach his men a lesson. He and Sergeant Evans went sneaking through the company position to steal rifles from sleeping men. The mission was successful; by daylight Sobel and Evans had nearly fifty rifles. With great fanfare, Evans called the company together and Sobel began to tell the men what miserable soldiers they were.[1]

What Sobel didn't realize was that the men he was berating weren't his own. He had wandered into the wrong camp and stolen the rifles belonging to Fox Company. Sobel didn't even realize his mistake until the commander of Fox Company came up with forty-five of his men.

The soldiers who served under Sobel mocked him and undermined him. By the time Easy Company began preparations for the invasion of Normandy, many men were taking bets on which of them would shoot Sobel when they finally joined the war in Europe. Fortunately, for both him and his men, Sobel was removed as company commander and reassigned before they went into combat.

Fortunately, most of Easy Company's leaders were excellent, and one in particular, who was awarded the Distinguished Service Cross, was considered by the men to be "the best combat leader in World War II."[2] That person was Dick Winters. He started out as a platoon leader in Easy Company during their training and was promoted to company commander after Normandy and later to battalion executive officer. He finished his brief military career with the rank of major.

Time after time, Winters helped his soldiers to perform at the highest level. And he always led from in front, setting the example, taking the risks along with them. Ambrose described Winters's philosophy of leadership in battle simply: "Officers go first."[3] Whenever his troops needed to assault an enemy position, Winters was in front leading the charge.

One of the most remarkable incidents demonstrating Winters's way of leading by example occurred soon after D-Day on the road to Carentan, a town that Easy Company needed to take from the Germans. As the American paratroopers under his command approached the town, they became pinned down by German machine-gun fire. Huddled in ditches on either side of the road, the soldiers froze and wouldn't move forward when ordered to. Yet if they didn't move, they would eventually be cut to pieces. Winters tried rallying them. He coaxed them. He kicked them. He ran from one ditch to the other as machine-gun bullets flew by. Finally, he jumped into the middle of the road, bullets glancing off the ground near him, and shouted at the men to get moving. Everyone got up and moved forward as one. And they helped to take the town.

More than thirty-five years later, Floyd Talbert, who was a sergeant, wrote to Winters about the incident and said, "I'll never forget seeing you in the middle of that road. You were my total inspiration. All my boys felt the same way."[4] In 2006, Winters summed up his approach to leadership, saying, "I may not have been the best combat commander, but I always strove to be. My men depended on me to carefully analyze every tactical situation, to maximize the resources that I had at my disposal, to think under pressure, and then to lead them by personal example."[5]

When Ambrose was asked what allowed Easy Company to distinguish itself during the war, to "rise above" its peers, Ambrose was clear in his response: "They weren't all that much better than other paratroopers, or the Rangers, or the Marines. They were one of many elite units in the war. But what made them special even among those who were already self-selected and special, was their leadership. . . . The great COs, platoon leaders and sergeants—not all elite units had such luck in their leaders, and that's the difference."[6] Why did that make such a difference? Because people do what people see. That is the Law of the Picture. When leaders show the way with the right actions, their followers copy them and can succeed.

OBSERVE

When times are tough, uncertainty is high, and chaos threatens to overwhelm everyone, followers are in greatest need of a clear picture from their leaders. They need a leader who embraces the Law of the Picture. The living picture they see in their leader produces energy, passion, and motivation to keep going.

1 What was the major difference in leadership style between Sobel and Winters?

_____

_____

_____

_____

_____

2 What made Winters a successful leader?

_____

_____

_____

_____

_____

3 Do you agree with the statement that people do what people see? Give an example.

_____

_____

_____

_____

_____

4 How has a leader in your organization or area of service is led by example?

_____

_____

_____

_____

_____

5 According to the Law of the Picture, how do leaders direct their teams to success?

_____

_____

_____

_____

_____

LEARN

Great leaders always seem to embody two seemingly disparate qualities. They are both highly *visionary* and highly *practical*. Their vision enables them to see beyond the immediate. They can envision what's coming and what must be done. Leaders possess an understanding of how . . .

- Mission provides *purpose*—answering the question, *Why?*
- Vision provides a *picture*—answering the question, *What?*
- Strategy provides a *plan*—answering the question, *How?*

As author Hans Finzel observed, "Leaders are paid to be dreamers. In fact, the higher you go in leadership, the more your work is about the future."[7]

At the same time, leaders are practical enough to know that vision without action achieves nothing. They make themselves responsible for helping their team members to take action. That can be difficult because the people who follow them often cannot envision the future as the leader does. They can't picture what's best for the team. They lose track of the big picture. Why? Because vision has a tendency to leak.

Leaders are stewards of the vision. So what should they do to bridge the vision gap between them and their followers? The temptation for many leaders is to merely communicate the vision. Don't get me wrong: communication is certainly important. Good leaders must communicate the vision clearly, creatively, and continually. The leader's effective *communication* of the vision makes the picture clear. But that is not enough. The leader must also *live* the vision. The leader's effective *modeling* of the vision makes the picture come alive!

That's not to say that leaders have all the answers. Anyone who has led anything knows that. The leaders who make the greatest impact are often those who lead well in the midst of uncertainty. Andy Stanley, an excellent leader and communicator, has addressed this issue. A few years ago at the Catalyst conference for leaders, he said:

Uncertainty is not an indication of poor leadership. Rather it indicates a need for leadership. The nature of leadership demands that there always be an element of uncertainty. The temptation is to think, *If I were a good leader, I would know exactly what to do.* Increased responsibility means dealing with more and more intangibles and therefore more complex uncertainty. Leaders can afford to be uncertain, but we cannot afford to be unclear. People will not follow fuzzy leadership.

MODELING INSIGHTS FOR LEADERS

If you desire to be the best leader you can become, you must not neglect the Law of the Picture. As you strive to improve as an example to your followers, remember these things:

1. THE PEOPLE YOU LEAD ARE ALWAYS WATCHING WHAT YOU DO

If you are a parent, you have probably already realized that your children are always watching what you do. Say anything you want, but your children learn more from what they see than from anywhere else. As parents, Margaret and I realized this early. No matter what we taught our children, they insisted on behaving like us. How frustrating. Legendary UCLA basketball coach John Wooden once quoted a poem that explains it perfectly:

> No written word
> > nor spoken plea
> Can teach our youth
> > what they should be
> Nor all the books
> > on all the shelves
> It's what the teachers
> > are themselves.[8]

Just as children watch their parents and emulate their behavior, so do employees watch their bosses. If the bosses come in late, then employees feel that they can too. If the bosses cut corners, employees cut corners. People do what people see.

Followers may doubt what their leaders say, but they usually believe what they do. And they imitate it. Former US Army general and secretary of state Colin Powell observed, "You can issue all the memos and give all the motivational speeches you want, but if the rest of the people in your organization don't see you putting forth your best effort every single day, they won't either."[9]

Whitley David asserted, "A good supervisor is a catalyst, not a drill sergeant. He creates an atmosphere where intelligent people are willing to follow him. He doesn't command; he convinces." Nothing is more convincing than living out what you say you believe.

2. It's Easier to Teach What's Right Than to Do What's Right

Writer Mark Twain quipped, "To do what is right is wonderful. To teach what is right is even more wonderful—and much easier." Isn't that the truth? It's always easier to teach what's right than it is to do it yourself. That's one of the reasons why many parents (and bosses) say, "Do as I say, not as I do."

One of my earliest challenges as a leader was to raise my living to the level of my teaching. I can still remember the day that I decided that I would not teach anything I did not try to live out. That was a tough decision, but as a young leader, I was learning to embrace the Law of the Picture. Author Norman Vincent Peale stated, "Nothing is more confusing than people who give good advice but set a bad example." I would say a related thought is also true: "Nothing is more *convincing* than people who give good advice and set a good example."

I once received calls on the same day about teaching ethics in the business arena from two reporters, one from the *Chicago Tribune* and the other from *USA Today*. Both asked similar questions. They wanted to know if ethics could be taught. My answer was yes.

"But many of the companies that teach ethics classes had ethics problems," one reporter pushed back.

"That's because ethics can be instilled in others only if it is taught *and modeled* for them," I replied. Too many leaders are like bad travel agents. They send people places they have never been. Instead, they should be more like tour guides, taking people places they have gone and sharing the wisdom of their own experiences.

John Wooden used to say to his players, "*Show* me what you can do; don't *tell* me what you can do." I believe team members have the same attitude toward their leaders. They want to *see* their leaders in action, doing their best, showing the way, and setting the example. V. J. Featherstone remarked, "Leaders tell but never teach until they practice what they preach." That is the Law of the Picture.

3. We Should Work on Changing Ourselves Before Trying to Improve Others

Leaders are responsible for the performance of the people they lead. The buck stops with them. They accordingly monitor their team members' progress, give them direction, and hold them accountable. And to improve the performance of the team, leaders must act as change agents. However, a great danger to good leadership is the temptation to try to change others without first making changes to yourself.

As a leader, the first person I need to lead is me. The first person that I should try to change and improve is me. My standards of excellence should be higher for myself than those I set for others. To remain a credible leader, I must always work first, hardest, and longest on changing myself. This is neither easy nor natural, but it is essential. In all honesty, I am a lot like Lucy in the *Peanuts* comic strip who tells Charlie Brown that she wants to change the world. When an overwhelmed Charlie Brown asks Lucy where she would start, her response is, "I would start with you, Charlie Brown. I would start with you."

Not long ago, I was teaching on the idea of 360-degree leaders, people who exert influence not just down with those they lead but also up with their boss and across with their colleagues. During a Q&A session, an attendee asked, "Which is the most difficult—leading up, across, or down?"

"None of the above," I answered quickly. "Leading myself is the toughest."

To lead any way other than by example, we send a fuzzy picture of leadership to others. If we work on improving ourselves first and make that our primary mission, then others are more likely to follow.

4. The Most Valuable Gift a Leader Can Give Is Being a Good Example

A survey conducted by Opinion Research Corporation for Ajilon Finance asked American workers to select the one trait that was most important for a person to lead them. Here are the results:

Rank	Characteristic	Percentage
1	Leading by example	26%
2	Strong ethics or morals	19%
3	Knowledge of the business	17%
4	Fairness	14%
5	Overall intelligence and competence	13%
6	Recognition of employees	10%

More than anything else, employees want leaders whose beliefs and actions line up. They want good models who lead from the front.

Leadership is more caught than taught. How does one "catch" leadership? By watching good leaders in action! When I think about my leadership journey, I feel that I have been fortunate to have had excellent leadership models from whom I have "caught" various aspects of leadership:

- I caught *perseverance* by watching my father face and overcome adversity.
- I caught *encouragement* by looking at how Ken Blanchard valued people.
- I caught *vision* by seeing Bill Bright make his vision become reality.

I continue to learn from good models, and I strive to set the right example for the people who follow me—my children and grandchildren, the employees in my companies, and the people who attend my conferences and read my books. Living what I teach is the most important thing I do as a leader. As Nobel Peace Prize winner Albert Schweitzer observed, "Example is leadership."[10]

DISCUSS

Answer the following questions and discuss your answers when you meet with your team.

1 How do vision and being practical work together in leadership?

_____

_____

_____

_____

2 How would you explain the statement, "Leaders can afford to be uncertain, but we cannot afford to be unclear"?

_____

_____

_____

_____

3 What is an example from your own experience of how a leader's actions have influenced you more than his or her words?

_____

_____

_____

_____

_____

_____

_____

_____

4 How much of your time is spent on personal growth compared to the time you spend investing in your team members?

_____

_____

_____

_____

_____

_____

_____

_____

5 How often do you find yourself imposing higher standards on others than you impose on yourself? How can you close the gap?

_____

_____

_____

_____

_____

APPLY

1 If you are already practicing the Law of Process, then you are currently working to sharpen your skills to increase your leadership ability. (If you're not, get started!) But there is more to leadership than just technical skills. Character is also vital to leadership, and that is communicated through the Law of the Picture. Your values and how you live them determine your character.

Give yourself a character audit. First, make a list of your core values, such as integrity, hard work, honesty, and so on. Then, think about your actions of the last month. What incidents, if any, stand out as inconsistent with those values? List as many things as you can recall. Don't dismiss anything too quickly, and don't rationalize any of your shortcomings. These items will show you where you need to work on yourself.

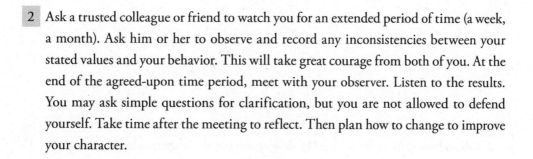

2 Ask a trusted colleague or friend to watch you for an extended period of time (a week, a month). Ask him or her to observe and record any inconsistencies between your stated values and your behavior. This will take great courage from both of you. At the end of the agreed-upon time period, meet with your observer. Listen to the results. You may ask simple questions for clarification, but you are not allowed to defend yourself. Take time after the meeting to reflect. Then plan how to change to improve your character.

3 What are the three to five things you wish your team members did better than they do now? List them. Now, grade *your performance* for each. (You may want to ask someone else to grade you as well to make sure your perception of yourself is accurate.) If your self-scores are low, then you need to change yourself in these areas before addressing them with others. If your self-scores are high, then you need to be more intentional about setting the example for your people.

_____

_____

_____

TAKE ACTION

Choose one area where you would like to see your team improve.

1 Why do you want your team to improve in this area?

_____

_____

_____

2 What will success look like?

_____

_____

_____

3 How will you improve yourself to reach your team goal? How will you model this behavior or skill to your team? How will you get the team involved?

_____

_____

_____

Determine a plan of action for the next few weeks or months. Set practical goals that will help to chart your progress. Remember to reward your team for reaching each goal.

14

❖ ❖

THE LAW OF BUY-IN

People Buy into the Leader,
Then the Vision

Many people who approach the area of vision in leadership have it all backward. They believe that if the cause is good enough, people will automatically buy into it and follow. But that's not how leadership usually works. People don't at first follow worthy causes. They follow worthy leaders who promote causes they can believe in. People buy into the leader first, then the leader's vision. Having an understanding of that will change your whole approach to leading people.

READ

In the fall of 1997, a few members of my staff and I had the opportunity to travel to India and teach four leadership conferences, something the organization would do many more times around the world in the decades since. That trip left a strong impression on me. India is an amazing country, full of contradictions. It's a place of beauty with warm and generous people. It was there that I was reminded of the Law of Buy-In.

I'll never forget when our plane landed in Delhi. Exiting the airport, I felt as if we had been transported to another planet. There were crowds everywhere. People on bicycles, in cars, on camels and elephants. People on the streets, some sleeping right on the sidewalks. Animals roamed free, no matter where we were. And everything was in motion. As we drove along the main street toward our hotel, I also noticed something else. Banners. Wherever we looked, we could see banners celebrating India's fifty years of liberty, along with huge pictures of one man: Mahatma Gandhi.

Today, people take for granted that Gandhi was a great leader. But the story of his leadership is a marvelous study in the Law of Buy-In. Mohandas K. Gandhi, called Mahatma (which means "great soul"), was educated in London. After finishing his education in law, he traveled back to India and then on to South Africa. There he worked for twenty years as a barrister and political activist. And in that time he developed as a leader, fighting for the rights of Indians and other minorities who were abused and discriminated against by South Africa's oppressive government.

By the time he returned to India in 1914, Gandhi was very well known and highly respected among his countrymen. Over the next several years, as he led protests and strikes around the country, people rallied to him and looked to him more and more for leadership. In 1920—a mere six years after returning to India—he was elected president of the All India Home Rule League.

The most remarkable thing about Gandhi isn't that he became a leader in India, but that he was able to change the people's vision for obtaining freedom. Before he began leading them, the people used violence in an effort to achieve their goals. For years riots against the British establishment had been common. But Gandhi's vision for change in India was based on nonviolent civil disobedience. He once said, "Nonviolence is the greatest force at the disposal of mankind. It is mightier than the mightiest weapon of destruction devised by the ingenuity of man."[1]

Gandhi challenged the people to meet oppression with peaceful disobedience and noncooperation. Even when the British military massacred more than one thousand people at Amritsar in 1919, Gandhi called the people to stand—without fighting back. Rallying everyone to his way of thinking wasn't easy. But because the people had come to buy into him as their leader, they embraced his vision. And then they followed him faithfully. He asked them not to fight, and eventually, they stopped fighting. When he called for everyone to burn foreign-made clothes and start wearing nothing but home-spun material, millions of people responded by doing it. When he decided that a March to the Sea to protest the Salt Act would be their rallying point for civil disobedience against the British, the nation's leaders followed him the two hundred miles to the city of Dandi, where government representatives arrested them.

Their struggle for independence was slow and painful, but Gandhi's leadership was strong enough to deliver on the promise of his vision. In 1947, India gained home rule. Because the people had bought into Gandhi, they accepted his vision. And once they had embraced the vision, they were able to carry it out. That's how the Law of Buy-In works. The leader finds the dream and then the people. The people find the leader, and then the dream.

OBSERVE

Every message people receive is filtered through the messenger who delivers it. If you consider the messenger to be credible, then you believe the message has value. That's one reason that actors and athletes are hired as promoters of products. People buy Nike shoes because they have bought into Cristiano Ronaldo, LeBron James, Serena Williams, and Tiger Woods, not necessarily because of the quality of the shoes.

1 Why did people buy into Gandhi's vision for non-violent protest? How had he established himself as a leader?

_____

_____

_____

_____

2 How do you think the people would have reacted to Gandhi's suggestion of non-violent protest if he had not already established himself as a leader?

_____

_____

_____

_____

3 Whose vision have you bought into? Why?

_____

_____

_____

4 Who in your profession or area of service seems to have the ability to rally people around their vision? What have they done to deserve such a response?

_____

_____

_____

_____

LEARN

You cannot separate leaders from the causes they promote. It cannot be done, no matter how hard you try. It's not an either/or proposition. The two always go together. Take a look at the following table. It shows how people react to leaders and their vision under different circumstances:

LEADER +	VISION =	RESULT
Don't buy in	Don't buy in	Get another leader
Don't buy in	Buy in	Get another leader
Buy in	Don't buy in	Get another vision
Buy in	Buy in	Get behind the leader

WHEN FOLLOWERS DON'T LIKE THE LEADER OR THE VISION . . . THEY LOOK FOR ANOTHER LEADER

The only time people will follow a leader they don't like with a vision they don't believe in is when the leader has some kind of leverage. That could be something as sinister as the threat of physical violence or as basic as the ability to withhold a paycheck. If the followers have a choice in the matter, they don't follow. And even if they don't have much of a choice, they start looking for another leader to follow. This is a no-win situation for everyone involved.

WHEN FOLLOWERS DON'T LIKE THE LEADER BUT THEY DO LIKE THE VISION . . . THEY LOOK FOR ANOTHER LEADER

You may be surprised by this. Even though people may think a cause is good, if they don't like the leader, they will go out and find another one. That's one reason that coaches change teams so often in professional sports. The vision for any team always stays the same: everyone wants to win a championship. But the players don't always believe in their leader. And when they don't, what happens? The owners don't fire all of the players. They fire the leader and bring in someone they hope the players will buy into. The talent level of most professional coaches is pretty similar. The effectiveness of their systems isn't that different. What often separates them from each other are their leadership and their level of credibility with players.

When Followers Like the Leader but Not the Vision . . . They Change the Vision

When followers don't agree with their leader's vision, they react in many ways. Sometimes they work to convince their leader to change the vision. Sometimes they abandon their point of view and adopt their leader's. Other times they find a compromise. But as long as they still buy into the leader, they rarely out-and-out reject him. They usually keep following.

An excellent example occurred in Great Britain. Tony Blair had a long tenure in office as prime minister. He was a popular leader, elected to serve three times. Yet at the same time, the majority of people in Great Britain were against Blair's policy of involving the nation in the war with Iraq. Why did Blair remain in office so long? Because they had bought into him as a leader. As a result, they were willing to live with their philosophical difference with him.

When Followers Like the Leader and the Vision . . . They Get Behind Both

When people believe in their leader and the vision, they will follow their leader no matter how bad conditions get or how much the odds are stacked against them. That's why the Indian people in Gandhi's day refused to fight back as soldiers mowed them down. That's what inspired the US space program to fulfill John F. Kennedy's vision to put a man on the moon. That's the reason people continued to have hope and keep alive the dream of Martin Luther King Jr., even after he was gunned down. That's what continues to inspire followers to keep running the race, even when they feel they've hit the wall and given everything they've got.

As a leader, having a great vision and a worthy cause is not enough to get people to follow you. You have to become a better leader. You must get your people to buy into you.

That is the price you have to pay if you want your vision to have a chance of becoming a reality. You cannot ignore the Law of Buy-In and remain successful as a leader.

DISCUSS

Answer the following questions and discuss your answers when you meet with your team.

1 How do leaders and followers differ when it comes to supporting a vision?

_____

_____

_____

_____

2 Under what circumstances would a follower look for another leader?

_____

_____

_____

_____

3 Why might you stay with a leader whose vision began to depart from what it was when you began following him or her?

_____

_____

_____

_____

4 Have you ever cast a vision and not had people buy into it and follow? How might your leadership have affected the response you received? Explain.

_____

_____

_____

_____

5   Up to now, did you approach leadership with the understanding that people must first buy into you before they will buy into your vision? Give an example of your previous leadership approach to casting vision and rallying followers.

_____

_____

_____

_____

APPLY

1   Do you have a vision for your leadership and your organization? What are you trying to accomplish? Write your thoughts in a vision statement. Is that vision worthy of your time and effort? Is it something you're willing to give a significant portion of your life to? (If not, rethink what you are doing and why.)

_____

_____

_____

_____

2   Has your team bought into you? If your team is small, list all of its members. If it is large, list the key players who influence the team. Now rate each person's buy-in on a scale of 1 to 10 (with 1 meaning they don't follow you, and 10 meaning they would follow you anywhere). Average those scores. If they're low, your people have not bought into you, and they will not help you execute your vision.

_____

_____

_____

_____

3 Think about ways you can earn credibility with each person on your team. There are many ways you can do that:

- Develop a better relationship.
- Be honest and authentic to develop greater trust.
- Set a good example.
- Help the person to become more successful.
- Help the person to achieve personal goals.
- Develop the person as a leader.

Develop a strategy with each person. If you make it your primary goal to add value to all of them, your credibility factor will rise rapidly.

TAKE ACTION

As a leader, you don't earn any points for failing in a noble cause. You don't get credit for being "right." Your success is measured by your ability to actually take the people where they need to go. But you can do that only if the people first buy into you as a leader.

Think about some problem, project or goal for which you have a vision. Then think about who could help you to realize that vision. During the coming weeks, intentionally build relationships with those people and do what you can to help them be successful. Only after you have invested in them should you share your vision. Once you have, note how they respond.

Vision: _____

Person who can help me realize my vision: _____

I will intentionally build a relationship with this person by:

_____

_____

Ways I can add value to him or her:

_____

The level of my connection before I shared my vision was _____

How this person responded to my vision:

_____

_____

_____

_____

15

THE LAW OF VICTORY

Leaders Find Ways for the Team to Win

Have you ever thought about what separates the greatest leaders who achieve victory from those who suffer defeat? What does it take to make a team a winner? It's hard to identify the quality that separates winners from losers. Every leadership situation is different. Every crisis has its own challenges. But I think that victorious leaders have one thing in common: they share an unwillingness to accept defeat. The alternative to winning is totally unacceptable to them. As a result, they figure out what must be done to achieve victory.

READ

Crisis seems to bring out the best—and the worst—in leaders because at such times, the pressure is intense and the stakes are high. That was certainly true during World War II when Adolf Hitler was threatening to crush Europe and remake it according to his vision. But against the power of Hitler and his Nazi hordes stood a leader determined to win, a practitioner of the Law of Victory: British prime minister Winston Churchill. He inspired the British people to resist Hitler and ultimately win the war.

Long before he became prime minister in 1940, Churchill spoke out against the Nazis. He seemed like the lone critic in 1932 when he warned, "Do not delude yourselves. . . . do not believe, that all Germany is asking for is equal status . . . They are looking for weapons and when they have them believe me they will ask for the return of lost territories or colonies."[1] As a leader, Churchill could see what was coming, and for years he tried to prepare the people of England for what he saw as an inevitable fight. But Prime Minister

Neville Chamberlain and the other leaders of Great Britain would not make a stand against Hitler. They were not prepared to do what it took to achieve victory. And more of Europe fell to the Nazis.

By mid-1940, most of Europe was under Germany's thumb. But then something happened that probably changed the course of history for the free world. The leadership of England fell to the sixty-five-year-old Winston Churchill, a courageous leader who had practiced the Law of Victory throughout his life. In his first speech after becoming prime minister, he said:

> We have before us an ordeal of the most grievous kind. We have before us many, many long months of struggle and of suffering. You ask, what is our policy? I can say: It is to wage war, by sea, land and air, with all our might and with all the strength that God can give us; to wage war against a monstrous tyranny, never surpassed in the dark, lamentable catalogue of human crime. That is our policy. You ask, what is our aim? I can answer in one word: Victory—victory at all costs, victory in spite of all terror, victory, however long and hard the road may be; for without victory, there is no survival.[2]

For more than a year, Churchill and Great Britain stood alone facing the threat of German invasion, defying Hitler. When Germany began bombing England, the British stood strong. Meanwhile, Churchill looked for ways to win and did everything in his power to prevail. He deployed troops in the Mediterranean against Mussolini's forces. Although he hated communism, he allied himself with Stalin and the Soviets, sending them aid even when Great Britain's supplies were threatened, and its own survival hung in the balance. And he developed his personal relationship with Franklin Roosevelt, hoping to develop an alliance with the president of the United States. In time his efforts paid off. On December 7, 1941, when the Japanese bombed Pearl Harbor, ushering the United States into the war, Churchill is said to have remarked to himself, "So we have won after all."

The stakes during the war were undoubtedly high. Pulitzer Prize–winning historian Arthur Schlesinger Jr. noted, "The Second World War found democracy fighting for its life. By 1941, there were only a dozen or so democratic states left on earth. But great leadership emerged in time to rally the democratic cause."[3] The team of Roosevelt and Churchill provided that leadership like a one-two punch. Just as the prime minister had rallied England, the president brought together the American people and united them in a common cause as no one ever had before or has since.

To Churchill and Roosevelt, victory was the only option. If they had accepted anything less, the world would be a very different place today. Schlesinger stated, "Take a look at our present world. It is manifestly not Adolf Hitler's world. His Thousand-Year Reich turned out to have a brief and bloody run of a dozen years. It is manifestly not Joseph Stalin's world. That ghastly world self-destructed before our eyes."[4] Without Churchill and England, all of Europe would have fallen. Without Roosevelt and the United States, it might never have been reclaimed for freedom. But not even an Adolf Hitler and the army of the Third Reich could stand against two leaders dedicated to the Law of Victory.

OBSERVE

When the pressure is on, great leaders are at their best. Whatever is inside them comes to the surface and works for or against them.

1 How do the words of Winston Churchill reflect the Law of Victory?

_____

_____

_____

2 How do the actions of Winston Churchill reflect the Law of Victory?

_____

_____

_____

3 How do you think Franklin Roosevelt's prior commitment to the Law of Victory factored into how he led America during World War II?

_____

_____

_____

4   Who is someone in your profession or area of service who reflects the Law of Victory? What does that person do that reflects that law?

_____

_____

_____

_____

LEARN

The Law of Victory is a factor on every type of team and in any kind of organization. Good leaders find ways for their teams to win in war, business, sports, education, non-profits, and politics. They recognize that there is a chance that victory can be won if three factors are present.

1. UNITY OF VISION

Teams succeed only when the players have a unified vision. No matter how much talent or potential there is, a team doesn't win a championship if its players are working from different agendas. That's true in professional sports. That's true in business. That's true in nonprofits.

I learned this lesson in high school when I was a junior on the varsity basketball team. We had a very talented group of kids, and many experts had picked us to win the state championship. But we had a problem. The juniors and seniors on the team refused to work together. They wouldn't even pass the ball to one another! They didn't look for ways for the *team* to win. It got so bad that the coach eventually gave up trying to get us to play together and divided us into two different squads for our games, one comprised of seniors, the other comprised of juniors. In the end the team had miserable results. Why? We didn't share a common vision. People played for the members of their class, not the team.

2. DIVERSITY OF SKILLS

It almost goes without saying that a team needs diversity in skills. Can you imagine a hockey team comprised entirely of goalies? Or a football team of quarterbacks? How about a business where there are *only* salespeople or nothing but accountants? Or a nonprofit organization with just fund-raisers? Or only strategists? It doesn't make sense. Every organization requires diverse talents to succeed.

Some leaders have blind spots in this area. In fact, I used to be one of them. I'm embarrassed to say there was a time in my life when I thought that if people would just be more like me, they would be successful. I'm wiser now and understand that every person has something to contribute. We're all like parts of the human body. For that body to do its best, it needs *all* of its parts, each doing its own job.

I recognize how each person on my team contributes using his or her unique skills, and I express my appreciation for them. The newer you are to leadership and the stronger your natural leadership ability, the more likely you will be to overlook the importance of others on the team. Don't fall into that trap.

3. A Leader Dedicated to Victory and Raising Players to Their Potential

It's true that having good players with diverse skills is important. As former Notre Dame head football coach Lou Holtz said, "You've got to have great athletes to win, I don't care who the coach is. You can't win without good athletes, but you can lose with them. This is where coaching makes the difference." In other words, you also require leadership to achieve victory.

Unity of vision doesn't happen spontaneously. The right players with the proper diversity of talent don't come together on their own. It takes a leader to make those things happen. It takes a leader to provide the motivation, empowerment, and direction required to win.

DISCUSS

Answer the following questions and discuss your answers when you meet with your team.

1 What are the three factors necessary for victory to be achieved?

_____

_____

_____

_____

2 Are there any other factors not mentioned in this list? If so, name them.

_____

_____

_____

3 Has anyone in your organization consistently demonstrated the Law of Victory? If so, in what ways?

_____

_____

_____

4 Which of the three factors for victory does your team strongly display? Explain.

_____

_____

_____

5 How can your team strengthen its unity of vision?

_____

_____

_____

6 As a leader, how can you express your dedication to victory?

_____

_____

_____

APPLY

1 The first step in practicing the Law of Victory is taking responsibility for the success of the team, department, or organization you lead. It must become *personal*. Your commitment must be higher than that of your team members. Your passion should be inexhaustible. Your dedication must be unquestioned.

Do you currently demonstrate that kind of commitment? If not, you need to examine yourself. If you search yourself and are unable to convince yourself to bring that kind of commitment, then one of three things is probably true:

- You are pursing the wrong vision.
- You are in the wrong organization.
- You are not the right leader for the job.
- You will have to make adjustments accordingly.

2 If you are dedicated to leading your team to victory, you will have your best shot at victory if you have the right people on the team. Think about all the skills necessary to achieve your goals. Write them down. Now compare that list with the names of the people on your team. If there are functions or tasks for which no one on the team is suited, you need to add members to the team or train the ones you have.

_____

_____

_____

_____

_____

3 The other crucial component for leading your team to victory is unity of vision. Do a little informal research to find out what's important to your team members. Ask them what they want to achieve personally. And ask them to describe the purpose or mission of the team, department, or organization. If you get a diversity of answers, you need to work on communicating a single vision clearly, creatively, and continually until everyone is on the same page. You should also work with each team member to show how personal goals can align with the team's overall goals.

_____

_____

_____

_____

TAKE ACTION

You and every person on your team have a unique set of gifts, talents, and training. This week, if your team has not done so already, take a personality test such as DISC or Myers Briggs. Then have each person, including yourself, fill out the survey below. Individually review each person's test and survey answers and then discuss with him or her the part he or she plays on the team. Also, let the team know about opportunities that are available to them to improve or learn specific skills.

1 What job task do you enjoy doing the most? Why?

_____

_____

_____

2 What job task do you least enjoy? Why?

_____

_____

_____

3 What are your hobbies and interests?

_____

_____

_____

4 What is your formal training (degrees, certifications, classes taken)?

_____

_____

_____

5 Outside of your obvious job skills, what other skills or training do you have?

_____

_____

_____

16

❖•❖•❖

THE LAW OF THE BIG MO

Momentum Is a Leader's Best Friend

If you've got all the passion, tools, and people you need to fulfill a great vision, yet you can't seem to get your organization moving and going in the right direction, you're dead in the water as a leader. If you can't get things going, you will not succeed. What do you need in such circumstances? You need to look to the Law of the Big Mo and harness the power of the leader's best friend: momentum.

READ

Several years ago I saw a movie called *Stand and Deliver* that illustrates the hopelessness many people feel in an organization without momentum. Maybe you've seen it too. It's about a real-life teacher named Jaime Escalante, a native of Bolivia, who worked at Garfield High School in East Los Angeles, California, and became the city's finest teacher.

At age forty-three, Escalante was hired by Garfield High School to teach computer science. But the school *had* no computers. Instead, they asked him to teach basic math classes, but he found that almost impossible because of the chaos he faced every day. Discipline was nonexistent. Fights broke out continually. Trash and graffiti were everywhere. Students—and even outsiders from the neighborhood—roamed all over the campus throughout the day. Gang activity was rampant. It was a nightmare.

He thought of quitting, but his passion for teaching and his dedication to improving the lives of his students wouldn't allow him to give up. And he was enough of a leader to know that the students were doomed if the school didn't change. They were all sliding backward fast, and they needed something to move them forward and start creating momentum.

Escalante believed that the way to improve the school was to challenge the school's best and brightest students with a calculus class that would prepare them for the AP exam that would earn them college credit. A few AP tests were already being given on campus in Spanish, and occasionally, a student might attempt a test in physics or history. But not math. The school didn't have a leader with vision to take up the cause. That's where Escalante came into play.

Escalante organized the first calculus class in 1978 with fourteen qualified students out of Garfield's 3,500 students. By the end of the second week of school, he had lost half of them. Even the ones who stayed were not well prepared for calculus, and by late spring, he was down to only five students. All of them took the AP test in May, but only two passed.

Escalante was disappointed, but he refused to give up. He knew that if he could help his students experience some wins, it would build their confidence and give them hope. He did whatever it took to motivate them. He wanted them to develop what he called *ganas*—desire.

The next fall, Escalante started another calculus class, this time with nine students. At the end of the year, eight took the test and six passed. Because his students were making progress, word of his success spread. Students heard that Garfield students were earning free college credit, and the class grew. In the fall of 1980, he had fifteen calculus students, fourteen of whom passed the AP test. Escalante's program was building momentum.

The next group of students, numbering eighteen, was the subject of the movie *Stand and Deliver*. Like their predecessors, they worked very hard to learn calculus, many coming to school at 7:00 a.m. every day—a full hour and a half before school started. And often they stayed until 5:00, 6:00, or 7:00 PM. And though Educational Testing Service (ETS) questioned the validity of the first test the students took, and they had to take it a second time, 100 percent of them passed.

After that, the math program had great momentum and it exploded. In 1983, the number of students passing AP calculus went from eighteen to thirty-one. The next year it doubled to sixty-three and continued growing. In 1987, eighty-five of Escalante's students received college credit for calculus. Garfield High School in East Los Angeles, once considered the sinkhole of the district, produced 27 percent of all passing AP calculus test scores by students of Mexican descent in the entire United States!

If that were the end of the story, that would be extraordinary. But the momentum created by Escalante in math created momentum for all of Garfield High School's students. The school started offering classes to prepare students for other AP exams. In time, Garfield held regular AP classes in Spanish, calculus, history, European history, biology, physics, French, government, and computer science with more than 325 students taking AP examinations. Places in the school became so coveted that Garfield had a waiting list of more than four hundred students from areas outside its boundaries wanting to enroll.

The school that was once the laughingstock of the district and almost lost its accreditation had become one of the top three inner-city schools in the entire nation![1] That's the power of the Law of the Big Mo.

OBSERVE

Momentum really is a leader's best friend because many times it's the only thing that makes the difference between losing and winning. When you have no momentum, even the simplest tasks seem impossible. Small problems look like insurmountable obstacles. Morale becomes low. The future appears dark. An organization with no momentum is like a train at a dead stop. It's hard to get going, and even small wooden blocks on the track can keep it from going anywhere.

On the other hand, when you have momentum on your side, the future looks bright, obstacles appear small, and troubles seem inconsequential. An organization with momentum is like a train that's moving at sixty miles per hour. You could build a steel-reinforced concrete wall across the tracks, and the train would plow right through it.

1 What obstacles did Escalante face at Garfield High School?

_____

_____

_____

_____

2 How did he create the momentum needed for the students to succeed and to grow the AP program?

_____

_____

_____

_____

3 How did the student body—not just those in his class—benefit from his actions?

_____

_____

_____

_____

4 What might have happened if the eighteen students hadn't retaken the test?

_____

_____

_____

_____

5 Is your organization or department currently experiencing positive momentum? Explain.

_____

_____

_____

_____

6 What obstacles to momentum are you currently facing?

_____

_____

_____

_____

7 What will it take to overcome them?

_____

_____

_____

_____

_____

LEARN

If you want your organization, department, or team to succeed, you must learn the Law of Momentum and make the most of it in your organization. Here are some things about momentum that you need to know:

1. MOMENTUM IS THE GREAT EXAGGERATOR

The Law of the Big Mo is easily seen at work in sports because the swings in momentum occur in the space of a few minutes right before your eyes. When a team gets on a roll, every play seems to work. Every shot seems to score. The team seems to do no wrong. The opposite is also true. When a team is in a slump, no matter how hard they work or how many solutions they try, nothing seems to work. Momentum is like a magnifying glass; it makes things look bigger than they really are. That's why I call it the great exaggerator. And it's one reason that leaders work so hard to create and use momentum.

Because momentum has such a great impact, leaders try to control it. In basketball games, for instance, when the opposing team is scoring a lot of unanswered points, a good coach will call a time-out. Why? He's trying to stop the other team's momentum before it becomes too strong. If he doesn't, the other team will likely run away with the game.

When was the last time you heard of a team on the cusp of winning a championship complain about injuries? Or second-guess their ability? Or totally rethink strategy? It doesn't happen. Is that because no one is injured and everything is perfect? No. It's because success is exaggerated by momentum. When you have momentum, you don't worry about small problems, and many larger ones seem to work themselves out.

2. Momentum Makes Leaders Look Better Than They Are

When leaders have momentum on their side, people think they're geniuses. They look past shortcomings. They forget about the mistakes the leaders have made. Momentum changes everyone's perspective of leaders. People like associating themselves with winners.

Young leaders often get less credit than they deserve. I often encourage young leaders not to lose heart. When leaders are new in their careers, they don't have any momentum yet. But once a leader creates some success for his organization and develops career momentum, then people give him *more* credit than he deserves. Why? Because of the Law of the Big Mo. Momentum exaggerates a leader's success and makes him look better than he really is. It may not seem fair, but that's just the way it works.

3. Momentum Helps Followers Perform Better Than They Are

When leadership is strong and there is momentum in an organization, people are motivated and inspired to perform at higher levels. They become effective beyond their hopes and expectations. That's what happened with the 1980 US Olympic hockey team. If you followed them—or if you've seen one of the movies made about them—then you know what I'm talking about. The team was good, but not good enough to win the gold medal. Yet that's what they did. Why? Because leading up to the championship game, they won game after game against very tough teams. They gained so much momentum that they performed beyond everyone's expectations. And after they beat the Russians, nothing could stop them from coming home with the gold medal.

The same kind of thing is true in business and nonprofit organizations. When an organization has great momentum, everyone working is more successful than they would be otherwise. Often they don't realize how much momentum helped them until they leave the organization to join another and suddenly their performance becomes merely average. When that happens, you know the Law of the Big Mo was at work. Even average people can perform far above average in an organization with great momentum.

4. Momentum Is Easier to Steer Than to Start

Have you ever been waterskiing? If you have, you know that it's harder to get up on the water than it is to steer once you're up there. Think about the first time you skied. Before you got up, the boat was dragging you along, and you probably thought your arms were going to give way as the water flooded against your chest and into your face. For a moment, you might have believed you couldn't hold on to the tow rope any longer. But then the force of the water drove your skis onto the surface, and off you went. At that point, you were able to make a turn with only a subtle shift of weight from one foot to another. That's the way the momentum of leadership works. Getting started is a struggle, but once you're moving forward, you can really start to do some amazing things.

5. Momentum Is the Most Powerful Change Agent

The story of Pixar is a classic example of the power of momentum. It changed the organization from an underfunded and understaffed organization scrapping to survive into an entertainment powerhouse. During the early days before it had momentum, the company considered creating hardware for medical companies so they could store and read MRIs. If that had happened, the organization would have lost its most talented and productive people. Instead, it transformed into an organization that has retaught Disney, the father of animated movies, how to regain its former glory.

Given enough momentum, nearly any kind of change is possible in an organization. People like to get on a winning bandwagon. Followers trust leaders with a proven track record. They accept changes from people who have led them to victory before. Momentum puts victory within reach.

6. Momentum Is the Leader's Responsibility

It takes a leader to create momentum. Followers can catch it. Good managers are able to use it to their advantage once it has begun. Everyone can enjoy the benefits it brings. But *creating* momentum requires someone who has vision, can assemble a good team, and motivates others. Creating positive change is the best way to prove you can lead others well. And everyone deserves to be led well.

If the leader is looking for someone to motivate him, then the organization is in trouble. If the leader is waiting for the organization to develop momentum on its own, then the organization is in trouble. It is a leader's responsibility to initiate momentum and keep it going. President Harry Truman once said, "If you can't stand the heat, get out of the kitchen." But for leaders, that statement should be changed to, "If you can't *make* some heat, get out of the kitchen."

7. MOMENTUM BEGINS INSIDE THE LEADER

Momentum begins within the individual leader. It starts with vision, passion, and enthusiasm. It starts with energy. Inspirational writer Eleanor Doan observed, "You cannot kindle a fire in any other heart until it is burning within your own."

If you don't believe in the vision and enthusiastically pursue it, doing all that you can to bring it to fruition, then you won't start making the small gains required to get the ball rolling to create momentum. However, if you model enthusiasm to your people day in and day out, attract like-minded people to your team, and motivate them to achieve, you will begin to see forward progress. Once you do, you will begin to generate momentum. And if you're wise, you'll value it for what it is: the leader's best friend. Once you have it, you can do almost anything. That's the power of the Big Mo.

DISCUSS

Answer the following questions and discuss your answers when you meet with your team.

1 How do leaders benefit from momentum?

_____

_____

_____

_____

2 How do followers benefit from momentum?

_____

_____

_____

3 Do you agree with the statement that "given enough momentum, nearly any kind of change is possible in an organization"? Explain.

_____

_____

4 How would you describe the momentum in your organization?

_____
_____
_____
_____
_____
_____

5 Who are the momentum makers in your organization? What have they done recently to create momentum?

_____
_____
_____
_____
_____
_____

6 What would create additional momentum in the organization?

_____
_____
_____
_____
_____
_____

7 What are you doing to become a momentum maker?

_____
_____
_____
_____
_____
_____

APPLY

1 Momentum begins inside the leader and spreads from there. Have you taken responsibility for the momentum where you lead? Are you passionate about the vision? Do you display enthusiasm? Do you encourage others? Do you find ways for your team to win? If you are a leader, these things are your responsibility.

_____

_____

_____

_____

_____

_____

2 Motivation is a key factor in developing momentum. The first step toward building motivation is removing demotivating elements within the organization. What is causing your team members to lose their passion and enthusiasm? How can you go about removing or at least minimizing those factors? Become your team's advocate.

_____

_____

_____

_____

_____

_____

3 To encourage momentum, you need to help your people celebrate their accomplishments. Make it a regular practice to honor people who "move the ball forward." Always praise effort, but *reward* only accomplishment. The more you reward success, the more people will strive for it.

_____

_____

_____

_____

_____

_____

TAKE ACTION

President Harry Truman once said, "If you can't stand the heat, get out of the kitchen." But for leaders, that statement should be changed to, "If you can't *make* some heat, get out of the kitchen." As the leader, you need to look for ways your team can experience wins by accomplishing goals. First, start with the smaller things you know they can achieve and gradually move them to larger goals that are more difficult. These accomplishments will build team momentum and allow your team to attempt and accomplish even more.

List the wins that your team will go after below. Start with the small goals and gradually move to larger goals. Be sure to celebrate each accomplishment as you achieve it to build morale.

Goals

1. _____
_____

2. _____
_____

3. _____
_____

4. _____
_____

5. _____
_____
_____

17

———◆◆———

THE LAW OF PRIORITIES

*Leaders Understand That Activity Is
Not Necessarily Accomplishment*

Leaders never advance to a point where they no longer need to prioritize. It's something that good leaders keep doing, whether they're leading a billion-dollar corporation, running a small business, pastoring a church, coaching a team, or leading a small group. I think good leaders intuitively know that to be true.

READ

Examine the lives of all effective leaders, and you will see them putting priorities into action. If you want to be an effective and successful leader, you will need to live according to the Law of Priorities. You must recognize that activity is not necessarily accomplishment. And if you want to go to the highest level, like the best leaders, you must get the Law of Priorities to work for you by satisfying multiple priorities with each activity, as they do. This actually enables them to increase their focus while reducing their number of actions.

A leader who was a master at that was one of my idols: John Wooden, the former head basketball coach of the UCLA Bruins. He was called the Wizard of Westwood because the amazing feats he accomplished in the world of college sports were so incredible that they seemed to be magical.

Evidence of Wooden's ability to make the Law of Priorities work for him could be seen in the way he approached basketball practice. Wooden claimed that he learned some of his methods from watching Frank Leahy, the great former Notre Dame head football coach. He said, "I often went to his [Leahy's] practices and observed how he broke them up into periods. Then I would go home and analyze why he did things certain ways. As a player, I realized there was a great deal of time wasted. Leahy's concepts reinforced my ideas and helped in the ultimate development of what I do now."

People who have served in the military say that they often have to hurry up and wait. That seems to be true in sports too. Coaches ask their players to work their hearts out one minute and then to stand around doing nothing the next. But that's not the way Wooden approached practice. He orchestrated every moment and planned each activity with specific purposes in mind. He employed economy of motion. Here's how he worked.

Every year, Wooden determined a list of overall priorities for the team, based on observations from the previous season. Those objectives might include items such as, "Build confidence in Drollinger and Irgovich," or "Use 3 on 2 continuity drill at least three times a week." Usually, he had about a dozen or so items that he wanted to work on throughout the season. But Wooden also reviewed his agenda for his teams every day. Each morning, he and an assistant meticulously planned the day's practice. They usually spent two hours strategizing for a practice that might not even last that long. Wooden drew ideas from notes jotted on three-by-five cards that he always carried with him. He planned every drill, minute by minute, and recorded the information in a notebook prior to practice. Wooden once boasted that if you asked what his team was doing on a specific date at three o'clock in 1963, he could tell you precisely what drill his team was running. Like all good leaders, Wooden always did the hard work of thinking ahead for the benefit of his team.

Wooden always maintained his focus, and he found ways for his players to do the same thing. His special talent was for addressing several priority areas at once. For example, to help players work on their free throws—something that many of them found tedious— Wooden instituted a free-throw shooting policy during scrimmages that would encourage them to concentrate and improve instead of just marking the time. The sooner a sidelined player made a set number of free throws, the sooner he could get back into the scrimmage. And Wooden continually changed the number of shots required of the guards, forwards, and centers so that team members rotated in and out at different rates. That way everyone, regardless of position or starting status, got experience playing with everyone else, a critical priority for Wooden's development of total teamwork.

The most remarkable aspect about John Wooden—and the most telling about his ability to focus on his priorities—is that he never scouted opposing teams. Instead, he focused on getting his players to reach *their* potential. And he addressed those things through practice and personal interaction with the players. It was never his goal to win championships or even to beat the other team. His desire was to get each person to play to his potential and to put the best possible team on the floor. And of course, Wooden's results were incredible. In more than forty years of coaching, he had only *one* losing season—his first. And he led his UCLA teams to four undefeated seasons and a record ten NCAA championships.[1]

Wooden was a great leader. He just might be the finest person to coach in any sport. Why? Because every day he lived by the Law of Priorities. We should strive to do the same.

OBSERVE

Not every leader practices the discipline of prioritizing. Why? I believe there are a few reasons. First, when we are busy, we naturally believe that we are achieving. But busyness does not equal productivity, and activity is not necessarily accomplishment. Second, prioritizing requires leaders to continually think ahead, to know what's important, to know what's next, to see how everything relates to the overall vision. That's hard work. Third, prioritizing causes us to do things that are at the least uncomfortable and sometimes are downright painful.

1 What did Wooden do to prepare for a team practice?

_____

_____

_____

_____

2 Why do you think Wooden was disinterested in scouting other teams?

_____

_____

_____

3 What is an example of how "activity is not necessarily accomplishment"?

_____

_____

_____

_____

4 How do you prepare so that you can maximize your effort?

_____

_____

_____

_____

5 Who in your organization or profession always seems to be "on track" with the right priorities? To what do you attribute that ability?

_____

_____

_____

_____

LEARN

Leaders can't afford to just think inside the box. Sometimes they need to reinvent the box—or blow it up. Executive and author Max De Pree said, "The first responsibility of a leader is to define reality." That requires the Law of Priorities. When you're the leader, everything is on the table.

Every year I spend about two weeks in December reevaluating my priorities. I review the previous year's schedule. I look at my upcoming commitments. I evaluate my family life. I think about my goals. I look at the big picture of what I'm doing to make sure the way I'm living aligns with my values and priorities.

One of the guiding principles I use during this process is the Pareto Principle. I've taught it for years, and I also explain it in depth in my book, *Developing the Leader Within You 2.0*. The idea is this: if you focus your attention on the activities that rank in the top

20 percent in terms of importance, you will have an 80 percent return on your effort. For example, if you have ten employees, you should give 80 percent of your time and attention to the best two. If you have one hundred customers, the top twenty will provide you with 80 percent of your business, so focus on them. If your to-do list has ten items on it, the two most important ones will give you an 80 percent return on your time and effort. If you haven't already observed this phenomenon, test it and you'll see that it really plays out that way. One year as I went through this process, I realized that I had to totally refocus and restructure one of my organizations.

The other guideline I use whenever I evaluate my priorities is the three Rs. No, not reading, writing, and 'rithmetic. My three Rs are requirement, return, and reward. I believe that to be effective, leaders must order their lives according to these three questions:

1. What Is Required of Me?

We're all accountable to somebody for the work we do—an employer, a board of directors, stockholders, the government, and so on. We also have responsibility for the important people in our lives, such as our spouse, children, and parents. For that reason, any list of priorities must begin with what is required of us.

The question I ask myself is, *What must I do that nobody can or should do for me?* As I have gotten older, that list has gotten shorter and shorter. If I'm doing something that's not necessary, I should eliminate it. If I'm doing something that's necessary but not required of me personally, I need to delegate it.

2. What Gives the Greatest Return?

As a leader, you should spend most of your time working in your areas of greatest strength. Marcus Buckingham and Donald O. Clifton have done extensive research on this subject, which you can read about in their book *Now, Discover Your Strengths*. People are more productive and more content when their work is within their natural gifting and strengths. Ideally, leaders should get out of their comfort zone but stay in their strength zone.

What's the practical application for this? Here's my rule of thumb. If something I'm doing can be done 80 percent as well by someone else, I delegate it. If you have a responsibility that someone else could do according to that standard—or that could *potentially* meet that standard—then develop and train a person to handle it. Just because you *can* do something does not mean that you *should* do it. Remember, leaders understand that activity is not necessarily accomplishment. That's the Law of Priorities.

3. WHAT BRINGS THE GREATEST REWARD?

This final question relates to personal satisfaction. Tim Redmond, president of Redmond Leadership Institute, observed, "There are many things that will catch my eye, but there are only a few things that will catch my heart."

Life is too short not to do some things you love. I love teaching leadership. I love writing and speaking. I love spending time with my wife, children, and grandchildren. I love playing golf. No matter what else I do, I will make time for those things. They are the fire lighters in my life. They energize me and keep me passionate. And passion provides the fuel in a person's life to keep him going.

REORDERING PRIORITIES

A few years ago when I went through this process of reprioritizing, I revisited the way I was spending my time and determined to allot my work time according to the following guideline:

Area	Time Allotted
Leadership	19 percent
Communicating	38 percent
Creating	31 percent
Networking	12 percent

These four areas represent my greatest strengths. They are the most rewarding aspects of my career. And they are also aligned with my responsibilities to my companies.

I realized as I was reviewing these areas that I was not maintaining the balance I desired. I was spending too much time in hands-on leadership at one of my companies, and it was taking away from higher priorities. Once again, I had to recognize that activity is not necessarily accomplishment. I knew I was in for another difficult business decision. If I was going to continue to be effective in fulfilling my vision, I would have to change and work according to the Law of Priorities. I made the decision to sell one of my companies. It wasn't easy, but it was the right thing for me to do.

DISCUSS

Answer the following questions and discuss your answers when you meet with your team.

1 Have you experienced the Pareto Principle, where you focused your attention on the activities that rank in the top 20 percent in terms of importance and you received an 80 percent return on your effort? Explain.

_____

_____

_____

_____

2 How does your organization delegate responsibilities?

_____

_____

_____

_____

3 How do you currently prioritize your responsibilities?

_____

_____

_____

_____

4 How can you make sure you always focus your greatest effort on your top 20 percent?

_____

_____

_____

_____

APPLY

1 Are you prepared to really shake up your life and get out of your comfort zone so that you can live and work according to your priorities? Pick an area of your life where your activity is high but your accomplishment isn't what it could or should be. What are you doing that you should not be doing? Eliminate it. What should you be delegating? Train someone to do it. What should you be doing that only you can do? Make it a priority.

_____

_____

_____

_____

2 If you have never done so before, take the time to write out your answers to the three R questions:

- What is required of me?
- What gives the greatest return?
- What brings the greatest reward?

Be sure to include family and other responsibilities, not just career. Once you have answered those three questions, create a list of the things you are doing that don't fit solidly into one of the three Rs. You need to delegate or eliminate these things.

3 Use the Pareto Principle to prioritize your daily activity. For the next two weeks, create a to-do list for the coming day and number the items in order of importance. The next day, begin with number one and work your way down the list. Your goal is *not* to complete the list every day. Your goal is to accomplish at least the top 20 percent of your list. At the end of three weeks, compare your productivity to your prior weeks' results.

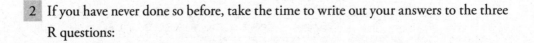

_____

_____

_____

_____

TAKE ACTION

It's easier to balance a schedule that has only a few things on it, but leaders and emerging leaders seldom have just a few things on their calendars. If you kept track of your events and project last year, look back at your calendar. If you didn't keep a detailed calendar, try to list the trips you took, projects you worked on, and daily tasks that made up your year. Answer the following questions by referring to that information.

1 What is required of me?

_____

_____

_____

2 What gives the greatest return?

_____

_____

_____

3 What brings the greatest reward?

_____

_____

_____

4 What tasks that do not bring a high return can I delegate to someone else?

_____

_____

_____

5 What tasks that do not bring a high return can be stopped altogether?

_____

_____

_____

6   How can I define my top 20 percent priorities?

_____

_____

_____

_____

7   How will I dedicate time, energy, and resources to these top priorities?

_____

_____

_____

_____

8   What rewards do I expect from focusing on my top priorities?

_____

_____

_____

_____

9   Who will I ask to keep me accountable to my top priorities? How often will we discuss my priorities?

_____

_____

_____

_____

18

•◆•

THE LAW OF SACRIFICE

A Leader Must Give Up to Go Up

There can be no success without sacrifice. Anytime you see success, you can be sure someone made sacrifices to make it possible. And as a leader, if you sacrifice, even if you don't witness the success, you can be sure that someone in the future will benefit from what you've given.

READ

Why does an individual step forward to lead other people? For every person the answer is different. A few do it to survive. Some do it to make money. Many desire to build a business or organization. Others do it because they want to change the world. That was the reason for Martin Luther King Jr.

King's leadership ability began to emerge when he was in college. He had always been a good student. In high school, he skipped ninth grade. And when he took a college entrance exam as a junior, his scores were high enough that he decided to skip his senior year and enroll in Morehouse College in Atlanta. At age eighteen, he received his ministerial license. At nineteen, he was ordained and received his bachelor's degree in sociology.

King continued his education at Crozer Seminary in Pennsylvania. While he was there, two significant things happened. He heard a message about the life and teachings of Mahatma Gandhi, which forever marked him. And he emerged as a leader among his peers and was elected president of the senior class. From there, he studied for his PhD at Boston University. It was also during this time that he married Coretta Scott.

King accepted his first pastorate in Montgomery, Alabama, at the Dexter Avenue Baptist Church in 1954, and settled into family life when his first child was born the next year in November. But that peace didn't last long. Less than a month later, Rosa Parks refused to relinquish her seat on a bus to a white passenger and was arrested. Local Black leaders arranged a one-day boycott of the transit system to protest her arrest and the city's segregation policy. When it was successful, they decided to create the Montgomery Improvement Association (MIA) to continue the boycott. Already recognized as a leader in the community, King was unanimously elected president of the newly formed organization.

For the next year, King led a boycott and negotiated with city leaders demanding courteous treatment of Black people by bus operators, first-come-first-served seating for all bus riders, and employment of Black drivers. He also helped community leaders to organize carpools, raise funds to support the boycott financially, mobilize the community, and coordinate legal challenges with the NAACP. Finally in November 1956, the US Supreme Court struck down the laws allowing segregated seating on buses.[1]

The Montgomery bus boycott was a major step in the American civil rights movement, and it's easy to see what was gained as a result of it. But King also began paying a personal cost for it. Soon after the boycott began, King was arrested for a minor traffic violation. A bomb was thrown onto his porch. And he was indicted on a charge of being party to a conspiracy to hinder and prevent the operation of business without "just or legal cause."[2]

Each time King climbed higher and moved forward in leadership for the cause of civil rights, the greater the price he paid for it. His wife, Coretta Scott King, remarked in *My Life with Martin Luther King, Jr.*, "Day and night our phone would ring, and someone would pour out a string of obscene epithets. . . . Frequently the calls ended with a threat to kill us if we didn't get out of town. But in spite of all the danger, the chaos of our private lives, I felt inspired, almost elated."

King did some great things as a leader. He met with presidents. He delivered rousing speeches that are considered some of the most outstanding examples of oration in American history. He led 250,000 people in a peaceful march on Washington, D.C. He received the Nobel Peace Prize. And he prompted change in this country. But the Law of Sacrifice demands that the greater the leader, the more he must give up. During that same period, King was arrested many times and jailed on many occasions. He was stoned, stabbed, and physically attacked. His house was bombed. Yet his vision—and his influence—continued to increase. Ultimately, he sacrificed everything he had. But what he gave up he parted with willingly. In his last speech, delivered the night before he was assassinated in Memphis, he said:

> I don't know what will happen to me now. We've got some difficult days ahead. But it doesn't matter to me now. Because I've been to the mountaintop. I won't mind. Like anybody else, I would like to live a long life. Longevity has its place. But I'm not concerned about that now. I just want to do God's will. And He's allowed me to go up to the mountain. And I've looked over and I've seen the Promised Land. I may not get there with you, but I want you to know tonight that we, as a people, will get to the Promised Land. So I'm happy tonight . . . I'm not fearing any man. "Mine eyes have seen the glory of the coming of the Lord."[3]

The next day, he paid the ultimate price of sacrifice.

OBSERVE

King's impact was profound. He influenced millions of people to peacefully stand up against a system and society that fought to exclude them. The United States is still in need of improvement, but it has changed greatly for the better because of his leadership.

1   What were some of the sacrifices that Martin Luther King Jr. made?

_____

_____

_____

_____

2   How did King's level of sacrifice increase as his influence increased?

_____

_____

_____

_____

3 How did King's sacrifice impact those who followed him? Those who opposed him?

_____

_____

_____

_____

4 What sacrifices have leaders in your profession or area of service made? Have those sacrifices paid off? Explain.

_____

_____

_____

_____

LEARN

There is a common misperception among people who aren't leaders that leadership is all about the position, perks, and power that come from rising in an organization. Many people today want to climb up the corporate ladder because they believe that freedom, power, and wealth are the prizes waiting at the top. The life of a leader can look glamorous to others on the outside. But the reality is that leadership requires sacrifice. A leader must give up to go up. In recent years, we've observed more than our share of leaders who used and abused their organizations for their personal benefit—and the resulting scandals that came because of their greed and selfishness. The heart of good leadership is sacrifice, not personal gain.

If you desire to become the best leader you can be, then you need to be willing to make sacrifices in order to lead well. If that is your desire, then here are some things you need to know about the Law of Sacrifice:

1. THERE IS NO SUCCESS WITHOUT SACRIFICE

Every person who has achieved any success in life has made sacrifices to do so. Many working people dedicate four or more years of their lives and pay tens or even hundreds of thousands of dollars to attend college to get the tools they'll need before embarking on their career. Athletes sacrifice countless hours in the gym and on the practice field preparing themselves to perform at a high level. Parents give up much of their free time and sacrifice their resources to do a better job raising their children. Philosopher-poet Ralph Waldo Emerson observed, "For everything you have missed, you have gained something else; and for everything you gain, you lose something."

Life is a series of trades, one thing for another. Leaders must give up to go up. That's true of every leader regardless of profession. Effective leaders sacrifice much that is good in order to dedicate themselves to what is best. That's the way the Law of Sacrifice works.

2. LEADERS ARE OFTEN ASKED TO GIVE UP MORE THAN OTHERS

The heart of leadership is putting others ahead of yourself. It's doing what is best for the team. For that reason, I believe that leaders have to give up their rights. As Gerald Brooks, leadership speaker and pastor, said, "When you become a leader, you lose the right to think about yourself." Visually, it looks like this.

When you have no responsibilities, you can do pretty much anything you want. Once you take on responsibility, you start to experience limitations in what you can do. The more responsibility you accept, the fewer options you have.

Digital Chairman and Chief Executive Robert Palmer said in an interview, "In my model of management, there's very little wiggle room. If you want a management job, then you have to accept the responsibility and accountability that goes with it."[4] He was really talking about the cost of leadership. Leaders must be willing to give up more than the people they lead.

For every person, the nature of the sacrifice may be different. Everyone who leads gives up other opportunities. Some people have to give up beloved hobbies. Many give up aspects of their personal lives. Some, like King, give their actual lives. The circumstances are different from person to person, but the principle doesn't change. Leadership means sacrifice.

3. YOU MUST KEEP GIVING UP TO STAY UP

Most people are willing to acknowledge that sacrifices are necessary early in a leadership career to make progress. They'll take an undesirable territory to make a name for themselves. They'll move their family to a less desirable city to accept a better position. They'll take a temporary cut in pay for greater opportunities for advancement. The problem for leaders comes when they think they have earned the right to stop making sacrifices. But in leadership, sacrifice is an ongoing process, not a one-time payment.

If leaders have to give up to go up, then they have to give up even *more* to *stay* up. Have you ever considered how infrequently sports teams have back-to-back championship seasons? The reason is simple: if a leader can win one championship with his team, he often assumes he can duplicate the results the next year by doing the same things. He becomes reluctant to make additional sacrifices in the off-season to prepare for what often turns out to be an even greater challenge the next year. But today's success is the greatest threat to tomorrow's success. And what gets a team to the top isn't what keeps it there. The only way to stay up is to give up even more. Leadership success requires continual change, constant improvement, and ongoing sacrifice. I found that to be true in my career. Before I founded my own companies and worked for myself, I took a pay cut every time I took a new position. It was a price I was willing to pay to grow and increase my influence.

4. The Higher the Level of Leadership, the Greater the Sacrifice

Have you ever been part of an auction? It's an exciting experience. An item comes up for a bid, and everyone in the room gets excited. When the bidding opens, lots of people jump in and take part. But as the price goes higher and higher, what happens? There are fewer and fewer bidders. When the price is low, everybody wants to bid. In the end, only one person is willing to pay the high price that the item actually costs. It's the same in leadership: the higher you go, the more it's going to cost you. And it doesn't matter what kind of leadership career you pick. You will have to make sacrifices. You will have to give up if you want to go up.

One time when I was speaking at a conference, someone came up to me during a break and said, "I want to do what you do." He was attracted to the influence and the excitement of speaking to a large audience. I appreciated his aspiration, but I couldn't help wondering, *But would you like to do what I did to be able to do what I do?* There was no way for him to know about the early days of speaking to nearly empty rooms; holding my first leadership conference and having so few people show up that it *cost* me money to go through with it; years of packing boxes with volunteers and hauling them to conference sites; being away from home and stranded in airports; working a full-time job in order to have the opportunity to build a career as a speaker; and all the rest that came with the territory. Maybe he did. I hope so, because a leader must give up to go up. That's the Law of Sacrifice.

DISCUSS

Answer the following questions and discuss your answers when you meet with your team.

1 What is the premise for the Law of Sacrifice?

_____
_____
_____
_____
_____

2 Do you agree that in order to move forward as a leader that you will have to give something up? Explain.

_____
_____
_____
_____
_____

3 Why do your rights decrease as your responsibilities increase?

_____
_____
_____
_____
_____

4 What is a recent example of something you had to give up in order to reach a goal that you set for yourself?

_____
_____
_____
_____

5 What have successful leaders in your organization given up in order to move forward or maintain their leadership?

_____

_____

_____

_____

_____

6 What one thing could you give up today that would move you closer to a goal you have set for yourself? Explain how you will commit to sacrificing this thing.

_____

_____

_____

_____

_____

_____

APPLY

1 To become a more influential leader, are you willing to make sacrifices? Are you willing to give up your rights for the sake of the people you lead? Give it some thought. Then create two lists: (1) the things you are willing to give up in order to go up, and (2) the things you are *not* willing to sacrifice. Be sure to consider which list will contain items such as your health, marriage, relationships with children, finances, and so on.

_____

_____

_____

_____

_____

2　Living by the Law of Sacrifice usually means being willing to trade something of value that you possess to gain something more valuable that you don't. King gave up many personal freedoms to gain freedoms for others. Rice gave up prestige and influence at Stanford to gain influence and impact around the world. What are you currently willing to trade in order to gain greater influence and lead positive change?

_____

_____

_____

_____

3　One of the most harmful mind-sets of leaders is "destination disease"—the idea that they can sacrifice for a season and then "arrive." Leaders who think this way stop sacrificing and stop gaining greater influence in their leadership.

　　In what areas might you be in danger of having destination disease? Write them down. Then for each, create a statement of ongoing growth that will be an antidote to such thinking. For example, if you have the mind-set that you have finished learning once you graduate from school, you may need to write, "I will make it my practice to learn and grow in one significant area every year."

_____

_____

_____

_____

TAKE ACTION

The Law of Sacrifice can be seen in almost any diet or financial plan. You stop eating certain things to lose weight. You don't go to the movies every weekend so you can take the family on vacation in the summer. And just like food and money, time is also a commodity. Earl Nightingale says that if a person studied one hour a day for three years on a single topic, that he or she would become an expert in that field. But what would that person have to give up in order to spend the time studying?

This week, you are to find one thing in your life that if you gave it up you believe it will move you forward. This is not limited to leadership. Moving forward might mean giving up your weekend golf game to spend more time with your family—investing in relationships. You could commit to waking up an hour earlier every morning to exercise—investing in your health. Or you could carve out one hour each day to learn about something that would advance your leadership and value to others—investing in your personal growth.

Fill in the blanks and commit to being committed!

For 6 months I will give up

_____

and instead I will

_____

My goal is to

_____

I will tell _____ about my progress and ask this person to keep me accountable.

19

---❖---

The Law of Timing

*When to Lead Is As Important As
What to Do and Where to Go*

When the stakes are high, the consequences of the Law of Timing are dramatic and immediate. Reading a situation and knowing what to do are not enough to make you succeed in leadership. If you want your organization, department, or team to win, you must pay attention to *timing*.

READ

A stark example of the importance of timing to leadership came to New Orleans in late August and early September of 2005. New Orleans is an unusual city. Like Venice, Italy, it is surrounded by water. To the north lies Lake Pontchartrain. To the south flows the mighty Mississippi River. To the east and west are low-lying swamplands. Canals crisscross the city. You cannot drive into or out of New Orleans without crossing a major bridge. That may not seem like a big deal—until you consider that most of the city lies below sea level. New Orleans is shaped like a bowl. On average, the city is six feet below sea level. In the lowest areas, it's nine feet below sea level. And the land in New Orleans sinks a little more every year. For decades citizens have worried about the potential damage that a direct hit from a powerful hurricane could do to the city.

On Wednesday, August 24, 2005, nobody in New Orleans could have known that the newly formed tropical storm, named Katrina, would be the big one—the hurricane the city

195

had feared would someday come. It wasn't until Friday that the National Hurricane Center predicted that the storm would reach landfall on Monday somewhere near Buras, Louisiana, about sixty miles southeast of New Orleans. The hurricane was already looking like a bad one. The next morning, Saturday, August 27, the leaders of many of Louisiana's parishes around New Orleans ordered mandatory evacuations: St. Charles, Plaquemines, parts of Jefferson, and even St. Tammany, which is situated on higher ground north of New Orleans.

But what about New Orleans? Why didn't Mayor Ray Nagin, the leader of the city, order a mandatory evacuation at the same time? Many people say New Orleanians are fatalistic, and they can't be made to move any faster than they want to go. Others say that Nagin, a businessman before he was elected, was worried about the legal and financial implications of an evacuation. I say he and others in government didn't understand the Law of Timing: when to lead is as important as what to do and where to go.

The right time to move people out of New Orleans was when the other parish leaders announced their mandatory evacuations. Nagin waited. On Saturday evening, he finally announced a *voluntary* evacuation of New Orleans. Only after Max Mayfield, the director of the National Hurricane Center, called Nagin on Saturday night did the mayor become concerned enough to act. "Max scared the crap out of me," Nagin is reported to have said after the call.[1]

The next morning at nine o'clock, Nagin finally ordered a mandatory evacuation— fewer than twenty-four hours before the hurricane would make landfall. It was much too late for many citizens of New Orleans. And how did he plan to help those people who couldn't make it out of town on such short notice? He advised them to make their way however they could to the Superdome, the city's shelter of last resort. But he made no real provisions for them. In a press conference Nagin advised:

> If you can't leave the city and you have to come to the Superdome, come with enough food, [non]perishable items to last for three to five days. Come with blankets, with pillows. No weapons, no alcohol, no drugs. You know, this is like the governor said, you're going on a camping trip. If you don't know what that's like, just bring enough stuff for you to be able to sleep and be comfortable. It's not going to be the best environment, but at least you will be safe.[2]

The results of Nagin's leadership played out in the national coverage of Katrina and its aftermath. Water was flowing into parts of the city by nine o'clock Monday morning.

Conditions for the people at the Superdome were dreadful. Other people who couldn't get out of town flocked to the Convention Center. Many citizens were stranded on rooftops. How did Nagin respond? He complained to the media at press conferences.

If someone was going to step in and lead, it would have to occur somewhere other than the local level. Most people began looking to the federal government for leadership, but its leaders violated the Law of Timing too. Not until Wednesday, August 31, did Director of Homeland Security Michael Chertoff release a memo declaring Katrina an "Incident of National Significance"—a key designation needed to trigger swift federal coordination.[3] President Bush didn't meet with his cabinet until the next day to determine how to launch the White House Task Force on Hurricane Katrina Response. Meanwhile, the people stranded in New Orleans waited for help. On Thursday, September 1, the Red Cross requested permission to take water, food, and supplies to the people who were stranded in the city, but their request was denied by the Louisiana office of Homeland Security. They were asked to wait another day.[4] Finally, on Sunday, September 4—six days after New Orleans had flooded—the evacuation of the Superdome was finally completed.

The way Katrina was handled shows leadership timing at its worst. It was botched at every level. Even the local animal shelter did better than the mayor. Two days prior to Katrina's arrival, it evacuated hundreds of animals to Houston, Texas.[5] In the end, 1,577 people from Louisiana died because of the hurricane.[6] Eighty percent of the deaths in Louisiana occurred in Orleans and St. Bernard parishes, with the overwhelming majority occurring in New Orleans.[7] If the leaders had paid greater attention not only to *what* needed to be done but also to *when* it needed to be done, many more lives would have been saved.

OBSERVE

Only the right action *at the right time* will bring success. Anything else exacts a high price. No leader can escape the Law of Timing.

1 | How did Mayor Nagin's hesitation impact the people he led?

_____

_____

_____

_____

2 How did the federal government violate the Law of Timing in their response to Katrina?

_____

_____

_____

_____

_____

3 Do you agree with the statement, "If the leaders had paid greater attention not only to what needed to be done but also to when it needed to be done, many more lives would have been saved"? Explain.

_____

_____

_____

_____

_____

4 How has the Law of Timing worked against someone in your profession or area of service?

_____

_____

_____

_____

_____

5 What is happening in your profession or industry now that will require attention to timing?

_____

_____

_____

_____

_____

LEARN

Good leaders recognize that *when* to lead is as important as what to do and where to go. Timing is often the difference between success and failure in an endeavor. Every time a leader makes a move, there are really only four outcomes:

1. The Wrong Action at the Wrong Time Leads to Disaster

A leader who takes the wrong action at the wrong time is sure to suffer negative repercussions. That was certainly the case in New Orleans as Katrina approached. Nagin's poor leadership set in motion a series of wrong actions at the wrong time. He waited until it was too late to call for a mandatory evacuation. He sent faxes to local churches, hoping they would help with evacuating people, but by the time he did, the people who would have received the faxes were already long gone. He picked a poor location for the shelter of last resort, neglected to supply it properly, and failed to provide adequate transportation for people to get there. One wrong action after another led to disaster.

Obviously, the stakes for every leadership decision are not as high as they were for Mayor Nagin. But every leadership situation requires that leaders heed the Law of Timing. If you lead a department or a small team and you take the wrong action at the wrong time, your people will suffer. If you repeatedly show poor judgment, even in little things, people start to think that having you as their leader is the real mistake.

And so will your leadership.

2. The Right Action at the Wrong Time Brings Resistance

When it comes to good leadership, having a vision for the direction of the organization or team and knowing how to get there aren't enough. If you take the right action but do it at the wrong time, you may still be unsuccessful because the people you lead will resist you. Good leadership timing requires many things:

- **Understanding**—leaders must have a firm grasp on the situation.
- **Maturity**—if leaders' motives aren't right, they'll pick timing that's best for themselves instead of the team.
- **Confidence**—people follow leaders who *know* what must be done.
- **Decisiveness**—wishy-washy leaders create wishy-washy followers.

- **Experience**—people trust experience, and if leaders don't possess it, they need to gain wisdom from others who do.
- **Intuition**—timing often depends on intangibles, such as momentum and morale.
- **Preparation**—if the conditions aren't right, leaders must create those conditions.

Having a handle on these factors improves a leader's timing.

3. THE WRONG ACTION AT THE RIGHT TIME IS A MISTAKE

People who are naturally entrepreneurial often possess a strong sense of timing. They intuitively know when it's time to make a move—to seize an opportunity. They sometimes make mistakes in their actions at those key moments. My brother Larry, who is an excellent businessman, has coached me in this area. Larry says that the greatest mistake made by entrepreneurs and other people in business is knowing when to cut their losses or when to increase their investment to maximize their gains. Their mistakes come from taking the wrong action at the right time.

Once again, I have experience in this area. Because I'm known primarily as a communicator, for years people tried to talk me into doing a radio program. For a long time I resisted the idea. In the mid-1990s, however, I could see there was a need for a growth-oriented program for people of faith. So we decided to create a program called *Growing Today*. But it had a problem: the format. Most programs of that type are supported by donations, but I believe in free-market economics. I wanted the program to support itself by selling products, the way any other commercial program would. What a mistake. The show never broke even. It was the right time, but the wrong idea. The Law of Timing had spoken again.

4. THE RIGHT ACTION AT THE RIGHT TIME RESULTS IN SUCCESS

When the right leader and the right timing come together, incredible things happen. An organization achieves its goals, reaps incredible rewards, and gains momentum. Success almost becomes inevitable. If you look at the history of nearly any organization, you will find a pivotal moment when the right leader took the right action at the right time, and it transformed the organization. Winston Churchill, whose greatness in leadership depended on the Law of Timing, described the impact that leaders can make—and the satisfaction they can experience—when they take the right action at the right time. He said, "There comes a special moment in everyone's life, a moment for which that person was born. That special opportunity, when he seizes it, will fulfill his mission—a mission for which he is uniquely qualified. In that moment, he finds greatness. It is his finest hour." Every leader desires to experience that moment.

DISCUSS

Answer the following questions and discuss your answers when you meet with your team.

1 What happens if you have the right idea but you implement it at the wrong time?

_____

_____

_____

_____

2 What happens if you know it's time to do something but choose the wrong thing to do? Give an example from your profession or area of service.

_____

_____

_____

_____

3 Do you agree with the statements that timing is just as important as what you do? Explain.

_____

_____

_____

_____

4 Up until now, how did you take timing into account when making a decision?

_____

_____

_____

5 How do you think examining the timing of a decision will affect your leadership in the future?

_____

_____

_____

_____

_____

6 What will you do to make sure—to the best of your ability—that your timing is right?

_____

_____

_____

_____

_____

APPLY

1 It has been said that managers do things right while leaders do the right things. The Law of Timing says that successful leaders do the right things at the right time. How much do you take timing into account as you lead? Do you think about the appropriateness of the timing as much as you do the rightness of the action? Review the major actions you've initiated in the past and discern whether you heeded the Law of Timing.

_____

_____

_____

_____

2 Spend some time analyzing a recent initiative that wasn't successful and characterize the actions and timing as wrong or right. To help you, answer the following questions:

- What was the goal of the initiative?
- Who was the individual responsible for leading it?
- What factors were taken into account while the strategy was planned?
- Whose experience did the strategy draw upon?
- What was the condition or temperature of the organization at the time of the launch?
- What were the market or industry conditions?
- What "leverage" was available and being used to aid in the initiative?
- What factors were clearly working against it?
- Might the initiative have been more successful had it been launched either earlier or later?
- Why did the initiative ultimately fail?

3 As you prepare to engage in future plans, use the list of factors from the lesson to prepare for the timing of your actions:

- **Understanding:** Do you have a firm grasp on the situation?
- **Maturity:** Are your motives right?
- **Confidence:** Do you believe in what you are doing?
- **Decisiveness:** Can you initiate action with confidence and win people's trust?
- **Experience:** Have you drawn upon wisdom from others to inform your strategy?
- **Intuition:** Have you taken into account intangibles such as momentum and morale?
- **Preparation:** Have you done everything you must do to set up your team for success?

Remember, only the right action at the right time will bring success to your team, department, or organization.

TAKE ACTION

Some of the most intriguing motives contain plots that are enhanced by using the Law of Timing. Murder mysteries, westerns, and action-adventure movies all rely on certain characters learning about what another character has done at a certain time, having the primary characters at a certain place at a certain time, and watching the hero take just the right steps at the right time in order to succeed.

This week, watch one of your favorite action movies. Take notes on how the Law of Timing played a role in success and failure.

1 Law of Timing moment:

_____

_____

_____

_____

2 What would have happened if the character had timed things differently?

_____

_____

_____

_____

20

❖❖❖

THE LAW OF
EXPLOSIVE GROWTH

To Add Growth, Lead Followers—
To Multiply, Lead Leaders

I haven't always felt the way I do now about leadership. My belief in the power of leadership and my passion for training leaders have developed over the course of my professional life. When I started in my career, I thought personal growth was the key to being able to make an impact. My father had been strategic in my development as I was growing up. He actually paid me to read books that he knew would help me, and he sent me to conferences when I was a teenager. Those experiences provided a great foundation for me. And after I began working, I discovered the Law of Process. That prompted me to take proactive ownership of my personal growth.

As a result, when people asked me to help them be more successful, I focused on teaching personal growth. It wasn't until I was forty years old that I began to understand the Law of the Inner Circle and the importance of developing a team. That's when my ability to grow an organization and reach greater goals began to increase. The greater the challenge you face as a leader, the greater the need for a good team. But my thinking went to a whole new level when I began to focus on adding and developing leaders to my team. When you recruit good, talented, capable followers to your team, you add to the team's ability. That has great value. But it doesn't compare to the impact of adding *leaders* to the team. That's why I say to add growth, lead followers—to multiply, lead leaders. That's the Law of Explosive Growth.

READ

The difference between teams of followers and teams of leaders became crystal clear to me in 1990 when I traveled to South America with my wife, Margaret, to teach leadership at a national conference. One of the great joys of my life is teaching leadership to people of influence. I love to add value to leaders who multiply value to others. I was really looking forward to this conference because it was an opportunity to add value to people outside my regular sphere of influence. But the experience didn't turn out the way I expected.

Everything started well at the conference. The people were gracious, and I was able to connect with them despite the language and cultural differences. But it wasn't long before I could tell that the attendees and I were not on the same page. When I started to teach about leadership, I could tell my comments were not connecting with them. They didn't engage, and what I was trying to communicate wasn't making an impact.

My evaluation of the situation was confirmed after my first session with them. As I spoke with individuals, they didn't want to talk about leadership issues. They didn't ask questions about growing their organizations or fulfilling a vision. They sought advice about personal issues, problems, and conflicts with other people. I felt that I was back doing personal counseling, similar to what I had done early in my career. For the next three days, I grew more and more frustrated. The people I spoke to didn't understand leadership, and they had no desire to learn about it. For someone like me who believes that everything rises and falls on leadership, I can't describe how much it frustrated me.

This wasn't the first time I had experienced this. When I had traveled to developing countries, I faced similar situations. In cultures where leaders are corrupt, honest people didn't want to become leaders. In nations without infrastructure, thriving businesses, or governments that support freedom, it is difficult for leaders to develop.

On the flight home after the conference, I expressed my frustrations to Margaret. I finally said, "I traveled thousands of miles just to counsel people on petty conflicts. If they would just turn their attention to becoming leaders, it would change their lives! I don't want to do this anymore."

After listening patiently, Margaret replied, "Maybe you're the one who's *supposed* to do something about this."

Margaret's exhortation to take action stirred something within me. In 1996, I brought together a group of leaders to help me create a not-for-profit organization to develop leaders in government, education, and the religious community, both in the United States and abroad. I named it EQUIP, which stood for Encouraging Qualities Undeveloped In People. EQUIP made modest progress in its goals, but in the months after the terrorist attacks of September 11, 2001, we went through a difficult period. We laid off half the staff and took the opportunity to reexamine our priorities.

We narrowed our focus. Moving forward, we would do one thing: train leaders internationally. And we developed a goal—one so large and daunting it looked almost impossible. We would try to develop *one million leaders* around the globe by 2008. How could a small nonprofit organization with a handful of employees hope to accomplish such a feat? By using the Law of Explosive Growth.

EQUIP's strategy, which came to be called the Million Leader Mandate (MLM), was to develop forty thousand leaders in countries around the world. We recruited leaders as volunteer trainers who would travel to countries at their own expense twice a year for three years to train leaders. With their help, EQUIP would provide all the training materials needed. In response, we asked those trained leaders to return to their own city, town, or village with training materials and personally train and develop twenty-five other leaders.

In 2002, EQUIP launched the MLM initiative, starting in India, Indonesia, and the Philippines. The response was overwhelming. Hundreds of hungry leaders traveled to each site to engage in the two-day training. Some attendees spent as many as five days *walking* to get to the events! And at the end of the training when we asked attendees to commit to developing twenty-five leaders over the next three years using the materials we would give them, more than 90 percent of the attendees signed on.

With the first success under our belt, we moved forward. The next year we began training leaders in other parts of Asia and the Middle East. In 2004, we started training in Africa; in 2005, Europe; and in 2006, South America. To our great surprise and delight, we reached our goal of training a million leaders two years ahead of schedule. Feeling we still were not done, we set a new goal, an even more audacious one: to develop five million leaders, and to train leaders from every one of the countries in the world that the United Nations recognized. In 2011, we accomplished that feat.

OBSERVE

No matter where you are, I know one thing. The best way for you to reach your potential, improve your team, help your organization, and make a difference is to attract, develop, and lead leaders rather than just followers. Leaders who develop leaders experience an incredible multiplication effect that can be achieved in no other way—not by increasing resources, reducing costs, increasing profit margins, improving systems, implementing quality procedures, or doing anything else. The only way to experience an explosive level of growth is to do the math—leader's math. That's the incredible power of the Law of Explosive Growth.

1 Why is it essential for your organization to develop leaders to experience growth?

_____

_____

_____

_____

2 What was the purpose of the Million Leader Mandate?

_____

_____

_____

3 What organization in your field has experienced explosive growth and sustained growth? How did they grow so quickly?

_____

_____

_____

_____

4 What is the current focus in your organization: leading leaders or followers? Explain.

_____

_____

_____

LEARN

All good leaders have vision. They can assess where their team or organization is, will project where it needs to go, and possess strong ideas about how their vision should be accomplished. They value action. They delight in progress. They want to move fast and see their vision fulfilled. And they continually feel a tension between where their organization *is* and where it *ought to be*.

I have experienced this tension my entire life. In every organization I've ever been a part of, I had a strong sense of where it should go. I even felt that way as a kid. (I wasn't always *right* about where we should go, but I always thought I *knew!*) How do you relieve the tension between where the organization is and where you want it to be? The answer can be found in the Law of Explosive Growth:

- If you develop yourself, you can experience personal success.
- If you develop a team, your organization can experience growth.
- If you develop leaders, your organization can achieve explosive growth.

It is possible to grow an organization and accomplish goals by leading followers. Many leaders do that. But if you want to maximize your leadership, help your organization reach its potential, and do that as quickly as possible, you must develop leaders. There is no other way to experience explosive growth. Adding other good leaders to a team is what I call leader's math. For every *follower* you add, you gain the talent and effort of one person. For every *leader* you add, you gain not only that individual's talent and effort, but also the talent and effort of all the other people he or she influences. That's multiplication!

A DIFFERENT FOCUS

Becoming a leader who develops leaders requires an entirely different focus and attitude from simply attracting and leading followers. It takes a different mind-set. Consider some of the differences between leaders who attract followers and leaders who attract and develop leaders:

Leaders Who Attract Followers . . . Need to Be Needed
Leaders Who Develop Leaders . . . Want to Be Succeeded

Becoming a leader can be exciting. When you speak, people listen. When you want to get something done, you can enlist other people to help you. Having people follow you can make you feel needed and important. However, that is a pretty shallow reason to pursue leadership. Good leaders don't lead for only themselves. They lead for the sake of others. They want to help their team members and they hope to create something greater than themselves, something that will last after their time of leadership has been completed.

Leaders Who Attract Followers . . . Develop the Bottom 20 Percent
Leaders Who Develop Leaders . . . Develop the Top 20 Percent

When you're leading a group of people, who typically asks for the most time and attention? The weakest members of the group who need the most help. If you allow them to, they will consume 80 percent or more of your time. However, proactive leaders who practice the Law of Explosive Growth don't invest most of their time in that bottom 20 percent. Instead, they seek out the top 20 percent in the group—the people with the greatest leadership potential—and they invest their time developing them. They know that if they develop the best, the best will help with the rest.

Leaders Who Attract Followers . . . Focus on Weaknesses
Leaders Who Develop Leaders . . . Focus on Strengths

How do you help people reach their potential? You focus on developing their strengths. Nobody ever became their best by focusing on their worst. That's why good leaders find their best people and help them develop what they're good at so that they can become even better. That can be hard to do when working with the bottom 20 percent. Most leaders who spend most of their time with people who don't perform well must focus on their weaknesses. Or they help them with the basics because problems in those areas keep them from achieving consistent performance on a regular basis. However, when you work with your best people, you can build on their strengths. And they can help those weaker than they are to develop.

Leaders Who Attract Followers . . . Treat Everyone the Same
Leaders Who Develop Leaders . . . Treat Individuals Differently

There is a myth in some leadership circles that promotes the idea of treating everyone on the team the same because it is the "fair" way to lead. What a mistake. As author

Mike Delaney said, "Any business or industry that pays equal rewards to its goof-offs and its eager beavers sooner or later will find itself with more goof-offs than eager beavers." Leaders who develop leaders give rewards, resources, and responsibility based on results. The greater the impact and influence leaders have, the greater the opportunities and resources they should receive. Why? Because they will make the most of them and get results.

Leaders Who Attract Followers . . . Spend Time with Others
Leaders Who Develop Leaders . . . Invest Time in Others

Leaders who attract only followers and never develop them to become leaders don't increase the value of those they lead. However, when leaders take time to develop the leaders they attract, they are making a valuable investment in them. Every moment they spend helps to increase their ability and influence. And that pays dividends to them, to their families, to the organization, and to the leader who developed them.

Leaders Who Attract Followers . . . Grow by Addition
Leaders Who Develop Leaders . . . Grow by Multiplication

As I've already mentioned, leaders who attract followers grow their organization only one person at a time. When you attract one follower, you impact one person. And you receive the value and power of one person. However, leaders who attract, develop, and lead leaders multiply their organization's growth, because every leader on their team brings along the value of everyone they influence.

Add ten followers to your organization, and you have the power of ten people. Add ten leaders to your organization, and you have the power of ten leaders times all of the followers and leaders they influence. That's the difference between addition and multiplication. It's like growing your organization by teams instead of by individuals.

Leaders Who Attract Followers . . . Impact Only People They Touch
Leaders Who Develop Leaders . . . Impact People Beyond Their Reach

Leaders who attract followers but never attract and develop leaders get tired. Why? Because they themselves must deal with every person under their authority. Being able to impact only the people you can touch personally is very limiting. In contrast, leaders who develop leaders impact people far beyond their personal reach. The better the leaders they develop, the greater the quality and quantity of followers and the greater the reach.

Every time you attract and develop leaders, helping them increase their leadership ability, you make them capable of influencing an even greater number of people. By helping one person, you can reach many others.

THE CHALLENGE OF LEADING LEADERS

If developing leaders has such a great impact, then why doesn't everyone do it? Because it's hard! Leadership development isn't an add-water-and-stir proposition. It takes a lot of time, energy, and resources. Here's why:

1. LEADERS ARE HARD TO FIND

How many people do you know who are really good leaders? They have influence. They can make things happen. They are able to see and seize opportunities. And they can attract, enlist, and rally people to perform with excellence. Not everyone is capable of doing that on a consistent basis. Most people are content to follow. Some are producers. Fewer are leaders. Leaders are like eagles—they don't flock. That's why they are so hard to find.

2. LEADERS ARE HARD TO GATHER

Once you find leaders, drawing them in can be very difficult. They are entrepreneurial and want to go their own way. If you try to recruit them, they want to know where you're going, how you plan to get there, who else you're planning to take with you—and whether they can drive! What you're doing has to be more compelling than what they're already doing without you.

On top of that, your organization needs to create an environment that is attractive to them. Most organizations desire stability, but leaders want excitement. Most organizations desire structure, but leaders want flexibility. Most organizations place a high value on following rules, but leaders often want to think and work outside the box. If you want to gather leaders, you must create a place where they can thrive.

3. LEADERS ARE HARD TO KEEP

As hard as it is to find and gather good leaders, it's even more difficult to keep them. The only way to lead leaders is to become a better leader yourself. If you keep growing and stay ahead of the people you lead, then you will be able to keep adding value to them. Your goal must be to keep developing them so that they can realize their potential. Only a leader can do that for another leader because it takes a leader to raise up another leader.

One year in my leadership conferences, I took an informal poll to find out what prompted the attendees to become leaders. The results were as follows:

Natural gifting	10 percent
Result of crisis	5 percent
Influence of another leader	85 percent

Only one leader in ten is able to blossom without the help of another leader. The rest need the help of other leaders who are ahead of them in the journey. If you keep adding value to the leaders you lead, then they will be willing to stay with you. Do that long enough, and they may never want to leave.

DISCUSS

Answer the following questions and discuss your answers when you meet with your team.

1 How would you define or describe "leader's math"?

_____

_____

_____

_____

_____

2 Why do some leaders prefer to lead followers instead of leading leaders?

_____

_____

_____

_____

_____

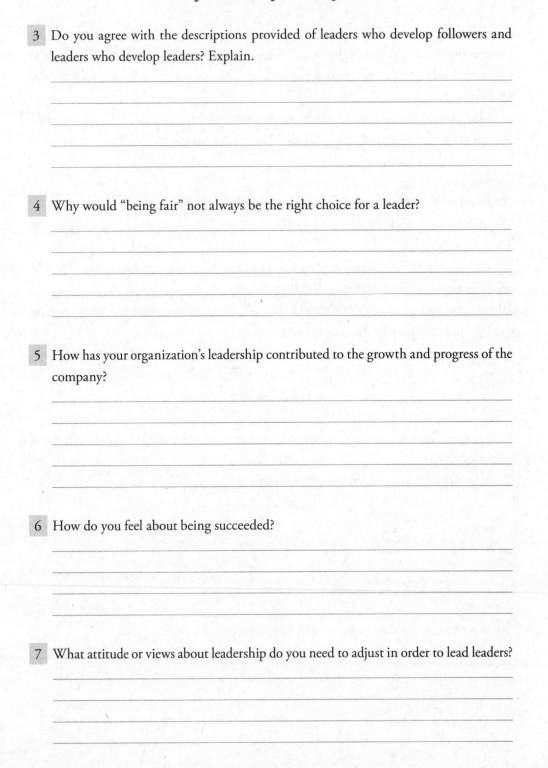

3　Do you agree with the descriptions provided of leaders who develop followers and leaders who develop leaders? Explain.

_____

_____

_____

_____

_____

4　Why would "being fair" not always be the right choice for a leader?

_____

_____

_____

_____

_____

5　How has your organization's leadership contributed to the growth and progress of the company?

_____

_____

_____

_____

_____

6　How do you feel about being succeeded?

_____

_____

_____

_____

7　What attitude or views about leadership do you need to adjust in order to lead leaders?

_____

_____

_____

_____

APPLY

1 What gives you greater personal satisfaction? Working with members of your team, solving problems with and for them, and enjoying the relationships? Or setting up team members to be independent leaders, giving them room to fail and succeed, and setting them up to be successful without you? If you want to harness the Law of Explosive Growth, you will need to lean into the latter. Prepare yourself emotionally to shift from being needed by team members to being succeeded by team members.

2 What are you currently doing to find and gather leaders? Are there places you go, events you attend, and networks you plug into to look for potential leaders? If not, get started. If so, what actions do you take to connect with leaders and recruit them for your organization, department, or team? How can you improve?

3 The way to hold on to leaders is to develop them and then set them up for success. Make sure you're doing the following to develop your leaders:

- Keep growing as a leader yourself so that you always have something to give to others.
- Create an environment where leaders can take chances, fail safely, succeed, and thrive.
- Invest most of your time in the top 20 percent of your leaders.
- Focus on developing your leaders' strengths.
- Treat every leader as an individual, matching investment, resources, and opportunities to their skills and abilities.

- Ask your best leaders to invest in other team members who are behind them in leadership.
- Celebrate your leaders' successes and encourage them to rise up to the next level.

TAKE ACTION

One of the keys to leading leaders is being able to identify a person's leadership potential. Dale Carnegie, a master at identifying potential leaders, once said, "Men are developed the same way gold is mined. When gold is mined, several tons of dirt must be moved to get an ounce of gold; but one doesn't go in to the mine looking for dirt—one goes in looking for the gold."

This week, use the following assessment to evaluate and identify the potential leaders on your team. These are the people you want to spend time investing in and developing to become future leaders for your organization.

0 = Never   1= Seldom   2 = Sometimes   3 = Usually   4 = Always

1. The person has influence.	0	1	2	3	4
2. The person has self-discipline.	0	1	2	3	4
3. The person has a good track record.	0	1	2	3	4
4. The person has strong people skills.	0	1	2	3	4
5. The person does not accept the status quo.	0	1	2	3	4
6. The person has the ability to solve problems.	0	1	2	3	4
7. The person sees the big picture.	0	1	2	3	4
8. The person has the ability to handle stress.	0	1	2	3	4
9. The person displays a positive spirit.	0	1	2	3	4
10. The person understands people.	0	1	2	3	4
11. The person is free of personal problems.	0	1	2	3	4
12. The person is willing to take responsibility.	0	1	2	3	4
13. The person is free from anger.	0	1	2	3	4
14. The person is willing to make changes.	0	1	2	3	4
15. The person has integrity.	0	1	2	3	4

16.	The person has a strong sense of self.	0	1	2	3	4
17.	The person has the ability to see what has to be done next.	0	1	2	3	4
18.	The person is accepted as a leader by others.	0	1	2	3	4
19.	The person has the ability and desire to keep learning.	0	1	2	3	4
20.	The person has a manner that draws people.	0	1	2	3	4
21.	The person has a good self-image.	0	1	2	3	4
22.	The person has a willingness to serve others.	0	1	2	3	4
23.	The person has the ability to develop other leaders.	0	1	2	3	4
24.	The person has the ability to bounce back when problems arise.	0	1	2	3	4
25.	The person takes initiative.	0	1	2	3	4

TOTAL POINTS _____

When assessing a potential leader, pay more attention to the quality of the person as addressed by the characteristics than to the specific score. Since leaders grade differently, scores vary. This is a general grading scale:

90–100   Great leader
80–89   Good leader
70–79   Emerging leader
60–69   Bursting with potential
Below 60 Needs growth but may not be ready to be mentored as a leader

Direct the 90–100 range people and ask them to mentor the 70–79 range people. Mentor the 80–89 range people yourself. Develop a leadership culture for the rest.

21

THE LAW OF LEGACY

A Leader's Lasting Value Is
Measured by Succession

What do you want people to say at your funeral? What do you want to see happen after you're gone? What do you want your legacy to be? These may seem like odd questions. But they may be the most important things you can ask yourself as a leader. Most people never consider it. And that's not good, because if they don't, their lives and leadership can take a direction different from that of their greatest potential and impact. If you want your leadership to really have meaning, you need to take into account the Law of Legacy.

READ

In the fall of 1997, I was in India with some colleagues, and we decided to visit the headquarters of a great leader of the twentieth century: Mother Teresa. Her headquarters, which the local people call the Mother House, is a plain concrete block building located in Kolkata. As I stood outside the doors, I thought that no one could tell by looking at it that this modest place had been the home base of such an effective leader.

We walked through a foyer and into a central patio that was open to the sky. Our intention was to visit Mother Teresa's tomb, which is located in the facility's dining room. But when we got there, we found out that the room was in use and we would not be allowed to go in until the ceremony was over.

We could see a group of about forty to fifty nuns seated, all dressed in the familiar habit that Mother Teresa had worn.

"What's going on in there?" I asked a nun passing by.

She smiled. "Today we are taking forty-five new members into our order," she said and then hurried away into another part of the building.

Since we were already running late and soon had to catch a plane, we couldn't stay. We looked around briefly and then left. As I walked out of the compound, through an alley, and among the throngs of people, I thought, *Mother Teresa would have been proud*. She was gone, but her legacy was continuing in others. She had made an impact on the world, and she had developed leaders who were carrying on her vision. And all appearances indicate that they will continue influencing people for generations to come. Mother Teresa's life is a vivid example of the Law of Legacy.

OBSERVE

In the end, our ability as leaders will not be measured by the buildings we built, the institutions we established, or the achievements of our team during our tenure. You and I will be judged by how well the people we invested in carry on after we are gone. As baseball great Jackie Robinson observed, "A life isn't significant except for its impact on other lives."

1 How would you describe Mother Teresa's legacy?

_____

_____

_____

_____

2 How does Mother Teresa's work continue to impact others?

_____

_____

_____

_____

3 Why did the work of Mother Teresa continue after her death?

_____

_____

_____

_____

_____

4 What organization similar to your own has had a significant leader leave? How did this affect the organization? Why?

_____

_____

_____

_____

_____

_____

LEARN

If you desire to make a leadership impact on a future generation, then I suggest that you become highly intentional about your legacy. I believe that every person leaves some kind of legacy. For some it's positive. For others it's negative. But here's what I know: we have a choice about what legacy we will leave, and we must work and be intentional to leave the legacy we want. Here's how:

1. Know the Legacy You Want to Leave

Most people simply accept their lives—they don't lead them. I believe that people need to be proactive about how they live, and I believe that is especially true for leaders. Grenville Kleiser, in his classic personal development book, *Training for Power and Leadership*, wrote:

> Your life is like a book. The title page is your name, the preface your introduction to the world. The pages are a daily record of your efforts, trials, pleasures, discouragements, and achievements. Day by day your thoughts and acts are being inscribed in your book

of life. Hour by hour, the record is being made that must stand for all time. Once the word "finis" must be written, let it then be said of your book that it is a record of noble purpose, generous service, and work well-done.[1]

Someday people will summarize your life in a single sentence. My advice: pick it now!

2. LIVE THE LEGACY YOU WANT TO LEAVE

I believe that to have any credibility as a leader, you must live what you say you believe. (I've touched on that in the Law of Solid Ground and the Law of the Picture.) Because my legacy involves adding value by influencing leaders, I have focused most of my attention on leaders, and I have become highly intentional in my efforts to lead them.

I believe there are eight major areas of influence in society: government, education, business, religion, media, arts, sports, and health care. In the early years of my career, I had influence in just one of those eight areas. I am constantly striving to reach and gain credibility in more of the others. I try to do that by building bridges, relating to people on a heart-to-heart level, and seeking to give more than I receive.

If you want to create a legacy, you need to live it first. You must become what you desire to give and see in others.

3. CHOOSE WHO WILL CARRY ON YOUR LEGACY

I've already mentioned this, but I want to reiterate it: a legacy lives on in people, not things. Max De Pree, author of *Leadership Is an Art*, declared, "Succession is one of the key responsibilities of leadership." Yet the Law of Legacy is something that few leaders seem to practice. Too often leaders put their energy into organizations, buildings, systems, or other lifeless objects. But only people live on after we are gone. Everything else is temporary.

There is often a natural progression to how leaders develop in the area of legacy, starting with the desire to achieve:

- **Achievement** comes when they do big things themselves.
- **Success** comes when they empower followers to do big things for them.
- **Significance** comes when they develop leaders to do great things with them.
- **Legacy** comes when they put leaders in position to do great things without them.

It's like my friend Chris Musgrove says, "Success is not measured by what you're leaving to, but by what you are leaving behind."

In 2011 when I cofounded the John Maxwell Team, I sensed that it was an opportunity to choose who would carry much of my legacy. By training and certifying speakers and coaches, I hoped that we would be creating "legs" for my legacy. And it has turned out even greater than I hoped. Today the JMT coaches are an army of more than forty thousand carriers of my DNA. They embrace my values, carry my principles, and add value to people in more than 150 countries around the work. And that army continues to grow! They are making a difference, and I believe 100 percent that they will continue doing so after I'm gone.

4. MAKE SURE YOU PASS THE BATON

Tom Mullins, an excellent leader and former coach who sits on EQUIP's board, tells me that the most important part of a relay race is the place that's called the exchange zone. That's where the runners must pass the baton to their teammates. You can have the fastest runners in the world—each one a record setter—but if they blow the exchange, they lose the race. The same is true when it comes to the Law of Legacy. No matter how well you lead or how good your successor is, if you don't make sure you pass the baton well, you will not leave the legacy you desire.

Tom knew this so well that for years he worked on his succession plan. He began early by grooming his son Todd, who is also an excellent leader, to take the baton and lead in his place. As time went on, Todd took on more and more responsibility until the baton was handed off completely to him. Tom tells me that his greatest joy now comes from seeing Todd and other leaders step up and do an even better job of leading than he did.

Just about anybody can make an organization look good for a moment—by launching a flashy new program or product, drawing crowds to a big event, or slashing the budget to boost the bottom line. But leaders who leave a legacy take a different approach. They take the long view. Author, educator, and theologian Elton Trueblood wrote, "We have made at least a start in discovering the meaning in human life when we plant shade trees under which we know full well we will never sit."

The best leaders lead today with tomorrow in mind by making sure they invest in leaders who will carry their legacy forward. Why? Because a leader's lasting value is measured by succession. That is the Law of Legacy.

DISCUSS

Answer the following questions and discuss your answers when you meet with your team.

1 Why are leaders who practice the Law of Legacy so rare today?

_____

_____

_____

_____

2 Why does an organization need a team of good leaders to succeed?

_____

_____

_____

_____

3 What does your organization's potential legacy look like? Who is involved in building that legacy?

_____

_____

_____

_____

4 What priority have you placed on mentoring others? Explain.

_____

_____

_____

_____

5 How would you go about choosing someone to replace yourself?

_____

_____

_____

6 If you suddenly left your organization, what would the impact be?

_____

_____

_____

_____

7 What will you do to ensure the legacy and future success of your organization?

_____

_____

_____

_____

APPLY

1 What do you want your legacy to be? If you are early in your leadership journey, I wouldn't expect you to have the definitive answer to that question yet. However, I still think there is value in your considering what you want your life to stand for. Take some time to think about your legacy. It will be closely related to your sense of purpose in life. It will use your gifts and skills. It will make use of your unique opportunities and personal circumstances. Who might you be able to impact, and how might you help others after your lifetime?

_____

_____

_____

_____

2 Based on your ideas about legacy, what must you change in the way you conduct yourself today so that you *live* that legacy? Write a list. It may include behavioral changes, character development, education, working methods, relationship building, and so on. The way you live will impact your ability to create the legacy you want to leave.

_____

_____

_____

3 In whom will you invest to carry on your legacy? Ideally, you should pick people with greater potential than your own who will be able to "stand on your shoulders" and do more than you did. Begin investing in them today.

_____

_____

_____

_____

TAKE ACTION

People invest in what they believe in. If you are just half-hearted about the organization you work for, it is unlikely that you will invest in that organization's future. Spend at least an hour today brainstorming and recording your thoughts about why you do what you do. At the end of this time, you may realize that you need to move into something that will better suit your gifts, talents, and the organization that you are willing to invest in. You may realize that you are right where you need to be, and that you should be investing in the vision and future of this organization. Or you may see how your current position is just a stepping-stone on your journey, but you can still invest by improving yourself as you try to strengthen the organization.

Some questions to get you started:

1 What does my organization provide for the community?

_____

_____

_____

2 Why is my organization important?

_____

_____

_____

3 Why do I believe in my organization's mission statement?

_____

_____

_____

_____

4 What job do I think I would most enjoy doing?

_____

_____

_____

_____

5 Why do I do what I do?

_____

_____

_____

_____

6 When all is said and done, what do I want my impact to be?

_____

_____

_____

_____

Conclusion

---◆◆---

EVERYTHING RISES AND FALLS ON LEADERSHIP

Well, there you have them—the 21 Irrefutable Laws of Leadership. Learn them, take them to heart, and apply them to your life. If you follow them, people will follow you. I've been teaching leadership for more than fifty years now, and during those years I've told the people I've trained something that I'm now going to say to you: everything rises and falls on leadership. The more you try to do in life, the more you will find that good leadership makes the difference. Any endeavor you can undertake that involves other people will live or die depending on the leadership. As you work to build your organization, remember this:

- **Personnel** determine the potential of the organization.
- **Relationships** determine the morale of the organization.
- **Structure** determines the size of the organization.
- **Vision** determines the direction of the organization.
- **Leadership** determines the success of the organization.

Now that you know the laws and understand them, share them with your team. And take time to evaluate yourself regarding each of the laws using the evaluation tool on the next pages. As I mentioned at the beginning of this book, nobody does all the laws well. That's why you need to build a team.

I wish you great leadership success. Pursue your dreams. Strive for excellence. Become the person you were created to be. Make a difference. And accomplish all that you were put on this earth to do. Leadership will help you to do that. Learn to lead—not just for yourself, but for the people who follow you. And as you reach the highest levels, don't forget to take others with you to be the leaders of tomorrow.

Appendix

SUGGESTIONS FOR LEADERSHIP GROWTH

For many years I have written books to add value to people. Now that you and your team have completed the leadership evaluation, I encourage you to use the following resources to enable you to lead yourself and others more efficiently.

1. THE LAW OF THE LID
Leadership Ability Determines a Person's Level of Effectiveness

The 21 Indispensable Qualities of a Leader
The Right to Lead
The 360-Degree Leader—Value #2: "Leaders Are Needed at Every Level of the
   Organization" and Value #4: "Good Leaders in the Middle Make Better
   Leaders at the Top"

2. THE LAW OF INFLUENCE
The True Measure of Leadership Is Influence—Nothing More, Nothing Less

Developing the Leader Within You—Chapter 1: "The Definition of Leadership:
   Influence"

The 360-Degree Leader—Section I: "The Myths of Leading from the Middle of an
Organization" and Section II: "The Challenges 360-Degree Leaders Face"
Winning with People

3. THE LAW OF PROCESS
Leadership Develops Daily, Not in a Day

Today Matters
Your Road Map for Success—Chapter 5: "What Should I Pack in My Suitcase?"
The 360-Degree Leader—Lead-Up Principle #9: "Be Better Tomorrow Than You
Are Today"
Leadership Promises for Every Day
The 21 Most Powerful Minutes in a Leader's Day

4. THE LAW OF NAVIGATION
Anyone Can Steer the Ship, but It Takes a Leader to Chart the Course

Developing the Leader Within You—Chapter 5: "The Quickest Way to Gain
Leadership: Problem-Solving"
Thinking for a Change—Skill 2: "Unleash the Potential of Focused Thinking";
Skill 4: "Recognize the Importance of Realistic Thinking"; Skill 5: "Release
the Power of Strategic Thinking"
Becoming a Person of Influence—Chapter 7: "Navigates for Other People"

5. THE LAW OF ADDITION
Leaders Add Value by Serving Others

Today Matters—Chapter 12: "Today's Generosity Gives Me Significance"
Thinking for a Change—Skill 10: "Experience the Satisfaction of Unselfish
Thinking"
Becoming a Person of Influence—Chapter 2: "Nurtures Other People"
The 360-Degree Leader—Lead-Up Principle #2: "Lighten Your Leader's Load";
Lead-Up Principle #3: "Be Willing to Do What Others Won't"; Lead-Across
Principle #3: "Be a Friend"; Lead-Across Principle #3: "Let the Best Idea Win"

Your Road Map for Success—Chapter 8: "Is It a Family Trip?" and Chapter 9: "Who Else Should I Take with Me?"

6. The Law of Solid Ground
Trust Is the Foundation of Leadership

Developing the Leader Within You—Chapter 3: "The Most Important Ingredient of Leadership: Integrity"
Becoming a Person of Influence—Chapter 1: "Integrity with People"
The 360-Degree Leader—Lead-Up Principle #1: "Lead Yourself Exceptionally Well"
Ethics 101

7. The Law of Respect
People Naturally Follow Leaders Stronger Than Themselves

Thinking for a Change—Skill 6: "Feel the Energy of Possibility Thinking" Your Road Map for Success—Chapter 4: "How Do I Get There from Here?"
Winning with People
The 360-Degree Leader

8. The Law of Intuition
Leaders Evaluate Everything with a Leadership Bias

Thinking for a Change—Skill 8: "Question the Acceptance of Popular Thinking" and Skill 11: "Enjoy the Return of Bottom-Line Thinking"
The 360-Degree Leader
Leadership Gold

9. The Law of Magnetism
Who You Are Is Who You Attract

Today Matters—Chapter 13: "Today's Values Give Me Direction"
The 360-Degree Leader—Lead-Across Principle #4: "Avoid Office Politics"

Talent Is Never Enough

The Choice Is Yours

10. THE LAW OF CONNECTION

Leaders Touch a Heart Before They Ask for a Hand

25 Ways to Win with People

The 360-Degree Leader—Lead-Up Principle #5: "Invest in Relational Chemistry";
   Lead-Across Principle #1: "Understand, Practice, and Complete the Leadership
   Loop"; Lead-Down Principle #1: "Walk Slowly Through the Halls"; Lead-
   Down Principle #2: "See Everyone As a '10'"

Becoming a Person of Influence—Chapter 8: "Connects with People"

Winning with People

11. THE LAW OF THE INNER CIRCLE

A Leader's Potential Is Determined by Those Closest to Him

The 17 Indisputable Laws of Teamwork

The 17 Essential Qualities of a Team Player

Teamwork Makes the Dream Work

The 360-Degree Leader—Lead-Down Principle #4: "Place People in Their
   Strength Zones" and Lead-Down Principle #7: "Reward for Results"

12. THE LAW OF EMPOWERMENT

Only Secure Leaders Give Power to Others

Failing Forward

The 360-Degree Leader—Lead-Across Principle #7: "Don't Pretend You're Perfect"

Winning with People—Section 1: "Are We Prepared for Relationships?" Becoming
   a Person of Influence—Chapter 9: "Empowers People" Thinking for a
   Change—Skill 9: "Encourage the Participation of Shared Thinking"

Your Road Map for Success—Chapter 6: "How Do I Handle the Detours?"

The Difference Maker

13. THE LAW OF THE PICTURE
People Do What People See

> The 360-Degree Leader—Lead-Down Principle #5: "Model the Behavior You Desire"
>
> Developing the Leader Within You—Chapter 6: "The Extra Plus in Leadership: Attitude" and Chapter 9: "The Price Tag of Leadership: Self-Discipline"
>
> Your Road Map for Success—Chapter 1: "The Journey Is More Fun if You Know Where You're Going" and Chapter 2: "How Far Can I Go?"

14. THE LAW OF BUY-IN
People Buy into the Leader, Then the Vision

> Developing the Leader Within You—Chapter 8: "The Indispensable Quality of Leadership: Vision"
>
> Your Road Map for Success—Chapter 3: "How Do I Get There from Here?"
>
> 25 Ways to Win with People Winning with People

15. THE LAW OF VICTORY
Leaders Find a Way for the Team to Win

> The 360-Degree Leader—Lead-Up Principle #8: "Become a Go-To Player"
>
> Thinking for a Change—Skill 1: "Acquire the Wisdom of Big-Picture Thinking" and Skill 3: "Discover the Joy of Creative Thinking"
>
> The Difference Maker

16. THE LAW OF THE BIG MO
Momentum Is a Leader's Best Friend

> Developing the Leader Within You—Chapter 4: "The Ultimate Test of Leadership: Creating Positive Change"
>
> The 360-Degree Leader—Lead-Up Principle #4: "Do More Than Manage—Lead!" and Lead-Up Principle #8: "Become a Go-To Player"

17. THE LAW OF PRIORITIES
Leaders Understand That Activity Is Not Necessarily Accomplishment

Developing the Leader Within You—Chapter 2: "The Key to Leadership: Priorities"

Today Matters—Chapter 4: "Today's Priorities Give Me Focus"

Thinking for a Change—Chapter 5: "Unleash the Potential of Focused Thinking"

The 360-Degree Leader—Lead-Up Principle #1: "Lead Yourself Exceptionally Well"

18. THE LAW OF SACRIFICE
A Leader Must Give Up to Go Up

Developing the Leader Within You—Chapter 3: "The Most Important Ingredient of Leadership: Integrity"

Your Road Map for Success—Chapter 7: "Are We There Yet?"

Today Matters—Chapter 8: "Today's Commitment Gives Me Tenacity"

Ethics 101—Chapter 5: "Five Factors That Can 'Tarnish' the Golden Rule"

19. THE LAW OF TIMING
When to Lead Is As Important As What to Do and Where to Go

The 360-Degree Leader—Lead-Up Principle #6: "Be Prepared Every Time You Take Your Leader's Time" and Lead-Up Principle #7: "Know When to Push and When to Back Off"

Thinking for a Change—Chapter 3: "Master the Process of Intentional Thinking" and Skill 10: "Embrace the Lessons of Reflective Thinking"

20. THE LAW OF EXPLOSIVE GROWTH
To Add Growth, Lead Followers—To Multiply, Lead Leaders

Developing the Leader Within You—Chapter 10: "The Most Important Lesson of Leadership: Staff Development"

Developing the Leaders Around You

Your Road Map for Success—Chapter 10: "What Should We Do Along the Way?"

Becoming a Person of Influence—Chapter 10: "Reproduces Other Influencers"

The 360-Degree Leader—Lead-Down Principle #3: "Develop Each Team Member as a Person"; Special Section: "Create an Environment That Unleashes 360-Degree Leaders"; Section VI: "The Value of 360-Degree Leaders"

21. THE LAW OF LEGACY

A Leader's Lasting Value Is Measured by Succession

The Journey from Success to Significance

Becoming a Person of Influence—Chapter 6: "Enlarges People"

The 360-Degree Leader—Lead-Down Principle #6: "Transfer the Vision"

Dare to Dream . . . Then Do It

NOTES

Lesson 1: The Law of the Lid

1. The Law of the Lid

Lesson 2: The Law of Influence

1. Thomas A. Stewart, "Brain Power: Who Owns It . . . How They Profit from It," *Fortune*, 17 March 1997, 105–6.
2. Paul F. Boller Jr., *Presidential Anecdotes* (New York: Penguin Books, 1981), 129.

Lesson 3: The Law of Process

1. "The Champ," *Reader's Digest*, January 1972, 109.
2. Milton Meltzer, *Theodore Roosevelt and His America* (New York: Franklin Watts, 1994).

Leson 4: The Law of Navigation

1. *Forbes*.
2. John C. Maxwell, *Thinking for a Change: 11 Ways Highly Successful People Approach Life and Work* (New York: Warner Books, 2003), 177–80.
3. Jim Collins, *Good to Great: Why Some Companies Make the Leap . . . and Others Don't* (New York: Harper Business, 2001), 86.

Lesson 5: The Law of Addition

1. Julie Schmit, "Costo Wins Loyalty with Bulky Margins," *USA Today*, 24 September 2004, http://www.keepmedia.com/pubs/USATODAY/2004/09/24/586747?extID= 10032 &oliID=213, accessed 24 August 2006.
2. Alan B. Goldberg and Bill Ritter, "Costco CEO Finds Pro-Worker Means Profitability," ABC News, 2 August 2006, http://abcnews.go.com/2020/Business/story?id=1362779, accessed 16 August 2006.
3. Barbara Mackoff and Gary Wenet, *The Inner Work of Leaders: Leadership as a Habit of Mind* (New York: AMACOM, 2001), 5.

4. Steven Greenhouse, "How Costco Became the Anti-Wal-Mart," *New York Times,* 17 July 2005, http://select.nytimes.com/search/restricted/article, accessed 22 August 2006.

5. Goldberg and Ritter, "Costco CEO Finds Pro-Worker Means Profitability."

6. Greenhouse, "How Costco Became the Anti-Wal-Mart."

7. Matthew 25:31–40 *The Message.*

Lesson 6: The Law of Solid Ground

1. Robert S. McNamara with Brian VanDeMark, *In Retrospect: The Tragedy and Lessons of Vietnam* (New York: Times Books, 1995).

2. Robert Shaw, "Tough Trust," *Leader to Leader,* Winter 1997, 46–54.

3. Russell Duncan, *Blue-Eyed Child of Fortune* (Athens: University of Georgia Press, 1992), 52–54.

4. Steve Balestrieri, "JFK Sends 400 Green Beret 'Special Advisors' in May 1961 to Begin Vietnam Involvement," SOFREP, May 25, 2017, https://sofrep.com/specialoperations/jfk -sends-400-green-beret-special-advisors-may-1961-begin-vietnam-involvement/.

5. C. N. Trueman, "John F. Kennedy and Vietnam," The History Learning Site, March 27, 2015, https://www.historylearningsite.co.uk/vietnam-war/john-f-kennedy-and-vietnam.

6. C. N. Trueman, "America and Vietnam (to 1965)," The History Learning Site, March 27, 2015, https://www.historylearningsite.co.uk/vietnam-war/america-and-vietnam-to -1965.

7. The Vietnam War," The History Place, https://www.historyplace.com/unitedstates /vietnam/index-1961.html, accessed August 17, 2012.

8. Robert S. McNamara with Brian VanDeMark, *In Retrospect: The Tragedy and Lessons of Vietnam* (New York: Times Books, 1995), 105.

9. McNamara and VanDeMark, *In Retrospect,* xvi.

10. Robert Shaw, "Tough Trust," *Leader to Leader*, Winter 1997, 46–54.

11. Russell Duncan, *Where Death and Glory Meet: Colonel Robert Gould Shaw and the 54th Massachusetts Infantry* (Athens: University of Georgia Press, 1999), 112.

12. Russell Duncan, *Blue-Eyed Child of Fortune* (Athens: University of Georgia Press, 1992), 52–54.

Lesson 7: The Law of Respect

1. M. W. Taylor, *Harriet Tubman* (New York: Chelsea House Publishers, 1991).

2. Based on the Bureau of Labor statistics, quoted in "Principal," Careers By the People, http://www.careersbythepeople.com/index/do/bio/, accessed 31 August 2006.

3. Based on the Bureau of Labor Statistics, quoted in "Principal," Careers By the People, http://www.careersbythepeople.com/index/do/bio/, accessed August 31, 2006.

Lesson 8: The Law of Intuition

1. Cathy Booth, "Steve's Job: Restart Apple," *Time,* 18 August 1997, 28–34.

2. Leander Kahney, "Inside Look at Birth of the iPod," *Wired,* 21 July 2004, http://www .wired.com/news/culture/0,64286–1.htm, accessed 1 September 2006.

3. Ana Letícia Sigvartsen, "Apple Might Have to Share iPod Profits," InfoSatellite.com, 8 March 2005, http://www.infosatellite.com/news/2005/03/a080305ipod.html, accessed 6 April 2006.

4. "iPod Helps Apple Quadruple Profit," BBC News, 10 December 2005, http://newsvote.bbc .co.uk, accessed 1 September 2006.

5. Lionel Sujay Vailshery, "Smartwatch Market Share By Vendor Worldwide 2014–2020," Statista [archived document], January 22, 2021, http://web.archive.org/web/202106180925 33/https://www.statista.com/statistics/524830/global-smartwatch-vendors-market-share/.

6. Kern Lima, 128.

Lesson 9: The Law of Magnetism

1. Reid Hoffman, "How to Unite a Team: Angela Ahrendts, Apple, Burberry," Masters of Scale, https://mastersofscale.com/angela-ahrendts/.

2. Our History," Burberry, https://uk.burberry.com/our-history/, accessed August 12, 2021.

3. Hoffman, "How to Unite a Team."

4. Angela Ahrendts, "Burberry's CEO on Turning an Aging British Icon into a Global Luxury Brand," *Harvard Business Review,* January-February 2013, https://hbr.org/2013/01 /burberrys-ceo-on-turning-an-aging-british-icon-into-a-global-luxury-brand.

5. Ahrendts, "Global Luxury Brand."

6. Hoffman, "How to Unite a Team."

7. Ahrendts, "Global Luxury Brand."

8. Ahrendts, "Global Luxury Brand."

Lesson 10: The Law of Connection

1. H. Norman Schwarzkopf, "Lessons in Leadership," vol. 12, no. 5.

Lesson 11: The Law of the Inner Circle

1. Michael Specter, "The Long Ride: How Did Lance Armstrong Manage the Greatest Comeback in Sports History?" *New Yorker,* 15 July 2002, http://www.newyorker.com /printables/fact/020715fa_fact1, accessed 15 September 2006.

2. Dan Osipow, "Armstrong: 'I'm More Motivated Than Ever,'" *Pro Cycling,* 23 June 2005, http://team.discovery.com/news/062205tourteam_print.html, accessed 15 September 2006.

3. "Cycling FAQ: Learn More About Team Discovery," Discovery Channel Pro Cycling Team, http://team.discovery.com/index.html?path=tabs3, accessed 15 September 2006.

4. Warren Bennis, *Scarce Organizing Genius: The Secrets of Creative Collaboration.*

LESSON 12: THE LAW OF EMPOWERMENT

1. Peter Collier and David Horowitz, *The Fords: An American Epic* (New York: Summit Books, 1987).

2. Lee Iacocca and William Novak, *Iacocca: An Autobiography* (New York: Bantam Books, 1984).

3. Lynne Joy McFarland, Larry E. Senn, and John R. Childress, *21st Century Leadership: Dialogues with 100 Top Leaders* (Los Angeles: Leadership Press, 1993), 64.

4. Acton Institute, "Lord Acton Quote Archive," https://www.acton.org/research/lord-acton-quote-archive, accessed February 23, 2022.

5. Lynne Joy McFarland, Larry E. Senn, and John R. Childress, *21st Century Leadership: Dialogues with 100 Top Leaders* (Los Angeles: Leadership Press, 1993), 64.

6. John Steinbeck, *Travels with Charley in Search of America* (New York: Penguin, 1986), Kindle, 55.

7. John Peers, Gordon Bennett, and George Booth, *1,001 Logical Laws* (New York: Doubleday, 1979), http://www.generationterrorists.com/quotes/1001l.html.

8. Erik Sherman, "23 Battle-Tested Leadership Quotes That Can Transform Your Life," *Inc*, May 25, 2015, https://www.inc.com/erik-sherman/23-battle-tested-leadership-quotes-that-can-transform-your-life.html.

9. Erik Sherman, "23 Battle-Tested Leadership Quotes That Can Transform Your Life," *Inc*, May 25, 2015, https://www.inc.com/erik-sherman/23-battle-tested-leadership-quotes-that-can-transform-your-life.html.

LESSON 13: THE LAW OF THE PICTURE

1. Stephen E. Ambrose, *Band of Brothers* (New York: Simon and Schuster, 2001), 36.

2. Dick Winters with Cole C. Kingseed, *Beyond Band of Brothers: The War Memoirs of Major Dick Winters* (New York: Penguin, 2006), front flap copy.

3. Ambrose, *Band of Brothers,* 38.

4. Ibid., 95–96.

5. Winters, Beyond Band of Brothers, 283.

6. Historian Stephen E. Ambrose, Author of 'Band of Brothers': The Story of Easy Company," Your Guide to U.S. Military, http://usmilitary.about.com/library/milinfo/band ofbrothers/ blbbambrose.htm, accessed 26 September 2006.

7. Author unknown, quoted in John Wooden with Steve Johnson, *Wooden: A Lifetime of Observations and Reflections On and Off the Court* (Chicago: Contemporary Books, 1997).

8. "Trouble Finding the Perfect Gift for Your Boss—How About a Little Respect?" 14 October 2003, Ajilon Office, http://www.ajilonoffice.com/articles/af_bossday_101403.asp, accessed 25 September 2006.

9. Oren Harari, *The Powell Principles: 24 Lessons from Colin Powell, Battle-Proven Leader* (New York: McGraw-Hill, 2005), 19.

10. "Albert Schweitzer Quotes," Brainyquote.com, https://www.brainyquote.com/authors /albert-schweitzer-quotes, accessed October 21, 2021.

LESSON 14: THE LAW OF BUY-IN

1. "Mahatma Gandhi: The Greatest Force at the Disposal of Mankind," Bartleby Research, https://www.bartleby.com/essay/Mahatma-Gandhi-The-Greatest-Force-At-The-F3ZNN 2VYAEFF, accessed August 20, 2021.

LESSON 15: THE LAW OF VICTORY

1. James C. Humes, *The Wit and Wisdom of Winston Churchill* (New York: Harper Perennial, 1994), 114.

2. Ibid., 117.

3. Arthur Schlesinger Jr., "Franklin Delano Roosevelt," *Time,* 13 April 1998.

4. Schlesinger, "Roosevelt."

LESSON 16: THE LAW OF THE BIG MO

1. Jay Mathews, *Escalante: The Best Teacher in America* (New York: Henry Holt, 1988).

LESSON 17: THE LAW OF PRIORITIES

1. John Wooden and Jack Tobin, *They Call Me Coach* (Chicago: Contemporary Books, 1988).

LESSON 18: THE LAW OF SACRIFICE

1. "Montgomery Improvement Association," King Encyclopedia, http://www.stanford.edu / group/King/about_king/encyclopedia/MIA.html, accessed 8 November 2006.

2. "Chronology of Dr. Martin Luther King, Jr.," The King Center, http://www.thekingcenter .org/mlk/chronology.html, accessed 8 November 2006.

3. David Wallechinsky, *The Twentieth Century* (Boston: Little, Brown, 1995), 155.

4. Hillary Margolis, "A Whole New Set of Glitches for Digital's Robert Palmer," *Fortune,* 19 August 1996, 193–94.

LESSON 19: THE LAW OF TIMING

1. David Oshinsky, "Hell and High Water," *New York Times,* 9 July 2006, http://www.nytimes.com/2006/07/09/books/review/09oshi.html?ei=5088&en=

4676642ee3fc7078&ex=1310097600&adxnnl=1&partner=rssnyt&emc=rss&adxnnlx=
1162847220-jiFf9bMhfwwKfuiWDA/Nrg, accessed 6 November 2006.

2. "New Orleans Mayor, Louisiana Governor Hold Press Conference" (transcript), CNN,
aired 28 August 2005, 10:00 a.m. ET, http://transcripts.cnn.com/TRANSCRIPTS/ 0508
/28/bn.04.html, accessed 6 November 2006.

3. Jonathan S. Landay, Alison Young, and Shannon McCaffrey, "Chertoff Delayed
Federal Response, Memo Shows," McClatchy Washington Bureau, 13 September 2005,
http://www.realcities.com/mld/krwashington/12637172.htm, accessed 2 November 2006.

4. "Red Cross: State Rebuffed Relief Efforts: Aid Organization Never Got into New Orleans,
Officials say," CNN, 9 September 2005, http://www.cnn.com/2005/US/09/08/ katrina
.redcross/index.html, accessed 2 November 2006.

5. Madeline Vann, "Search and Rescue," *Tulanian,* Summer 2006, http://www2.tulane.edu
/ article_news_details.cfm?ArticleID=6752, accessed 7 November 2006.

6. "Hurricane Katrina," http://www.answers.com/topic/hurricane-katrina, accessed 7
November 2006.

7. Coleman Warner and Robert Travis Scott, "Where They Died," *Times-Picayune,* 23
October 2005, http://pqasb.pqarchiver.com/timespicayune/access/915268571.htm
l?dids=915268571:915268571&FMT=ABS&FMTS=ABS:FT&date=Oct+23%2C+
2005&author=Coleman+Warner+and+Robert+Travis+Scott+Staff+writers&pub=Ti
mes+-+Picayune&edition=&startpage=01&desc=WHERE+THEY+DIED+, accessed 7
November 2006.

LESSON 21: THE LAW OF LEGACY

1. Question and Answer Session with Truett Cathy and Dan Cathy, Exchange [Conference],
2 November 2005.

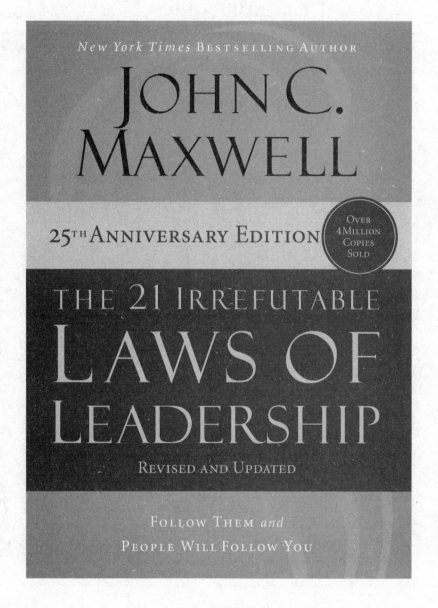
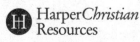

LEADERSHIP FOUNDATION

transforming
LEADERS

transforming
COUNTRIES

Together,
WE CAN CHANGE THE WORLD.
jmlf.org

THE JOHN
MAXWELL
**LEADERSHIP
BLOG**

Every week John Maxwell
and CEO of The John Maxwell Enterprise, Mark Cole,
share their in-the-moment thoughts on leadership
and how to navigate your personal growth journey
week by week.

CHECK IT OUT AT **JOHNMAXWELL.COM/BLOG**

LEADERSHIP IS TAUGHT.
DEVELOP THE LEADERS WITHIN YOUR COMPANY.

When you begin to invest in your human capital, watch what happens. Your workforce becomes aligned with your corporate initiatives. They begin supporting critical business priorities and change efforts, AND your business success begins to accelerate.

LEADERSHIP DEVELOPMENT

EMPLOYEE ENGAGEMENT

CHANGE MANAGEMENT